Polar Bears
Outstanding Survivors of Climate Change

SUSAN J. CROCKFORD

Copyright © 2017 Susan J. Crockford

All rights reserved.

ISBN: 1541139712
ISBN-13: 978-1541139718

CONTENTS

	About me	i
	About this book	ii
1	Polar bear & sea ice basics	1
2	Feasting/fasting life of polar bears	9
3	Evolution & climate change	13
4	Conservation & protection	15
5	Failure of the polar bear predictions	17
6	Biggest threat to polar bears	21
7	Summary	27
8	Conclusions	29
	References by page number & topic	31
	Photo & figure credits	46
	Glossary	47
	Acknowledgements	48

About Me

I am an active professional zoologist with specialties in the identification of ancient animal remains and animal ecology, as well as species evolution and adaptation.

For more than 25 years, I have been investigating the ecology and evolution of polar bears, in addition to other vertebrate species (dogs, wolves, bluefin tuna, shorttailed albatross, mountain goats, northern fur seals, Steller sea lions, and Arctic ringed seals) – see www.pacificid.com for a complete list.

My scientific background includes a solid foundation in the mechanisms of evolution, the fossil and archaeological records, the geological history of Arctic sea ice, and the ecological and genetic evidence of living species necessary for understanding their history.

Over the years, I have written a number of scientific papers on a wide range of topics, including human colonization of the Arctic – see www.pacificid.com for this list.

My Ph.D. dissertation (2004) examined the origin of domestic dogs as well as polar bears and showed how evolution actually works; my book *Rhythms of Life: Thyroid Hormone and the Origin of Species* is a version of that work for general readers.

This broad spectrum science background gives me a big picture perspective on contemporary polar bear issues that researchers specialized in data collection and modeling survival are lacking. I've recently published a paper on predictions of summer sea ice and polar bear survival (Crockford 2017).

Since August 2012, I have been writing a popular science blog called Polar Bear Science (www.polarbearscience.com). The blog's focus is on polar bear ecology of the past and present – without spin, advocacy, or politics. I am a scientist – I leave prognostications about the future to fortune-tellers except when I am writing fiction, in which case I identify it as such (e.g., *EATEN: A novel*). Find my book website at www.susancrockford.com.

About this Book

This concise digest is styled after a popular lecture I have presented since 2009 through the University of Victoria's Speakers Bureau (updated over the years, of course) which has always been well received. The opinions expressed in those lectures, and in this book, are my own and do not necessarily reflect those of the University of Victoria or any other agencies that have supported my research.

I have purposely kept the book short so that full-color images could be included because they speak volumes. The information provided here is based on peer-reviewed literature (except where noted otherwise)' however, to keep the format simple, references are not cited in the text but are listed at the end of the book by page number (and sometimes, within the page, by topic).

I hope you will find the diverse background and broad perspective I bring to the field of polar bear science to be a refreshing addition. Here, I have endeavored to lay out, as simply as possible, the relevant science necessary for understanding polar bear ecology and population health, in the context of long term conservation concerns. This has meant addressing inconvenient topics, including reconciling doomsday predictions against recent observations.

It is not my intension to criticize the valuable effort that field researchers have contributed to polar bear science, but I do take issue with those who insist that being a collector of polar bear data makes their opinion the final word regarding its interpretation and significance.

Further detail on topics mentioned here can be found at www.polarbearscience.com where you will also find a contact-me form. I will gladly pass along additional information on request.

Chapter 1   Polar Bear & Sea Ice Basics

Where polar bears live

The area of polar bear habitat equals the approximate extent of Arctic sea ice in March (the yearly maximum), with three important exceptions. Three areas have sea ice in winter but no polar bears: Okhotsk Sea (OS), Baltic Sea (BS), and the Gulf of St. Lawrence (GSL). If all three were filled with ice, together they would represent 2.4 mkm² of the total Arctic extent total (Fig. 1). If we remove these areas of sea ice from the Arctic extent totals for the satellite record (1979-2016), total polar bear habitat at the end of March has been virtually constant at about 14.0 mkm² per year.

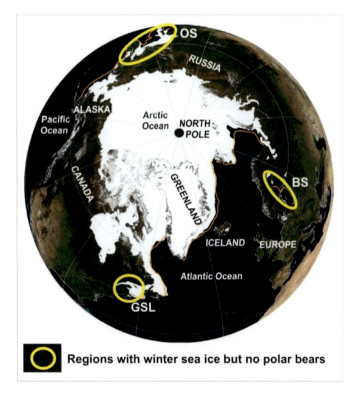

Figure 1. Global polar bear habitat is the approximate extent of sea ice in winter (2016) with three important exceptions: the Baltic Sea (BS), the Okhotsk Sea (OS) and the Gulf of St. Lawrence (GSL).

There is no evidence that polar bears ever lived in the Okhotsk Sea or the Baltic Sea. But while there were occasional reports of bears in the Gulf of St. Lawrence into the early 1900s, none exist there today. Polar bears are currently well distributed throughout their available habitat, despite recent changes in sea ice coverage: there have been no range contractions due to reduced habitat.

Polar bears live primarily around the edge of the Arctic Ocean, in the so-called peripheral seas that lie off the land masses of the Northern Hemisphere, which include the enormous Hudson Bay basin (Fig. 2). These peripheral seas are often broad expanses of water less than 300m deep that are covered in relatively thin, first year ice (2-3 m thick) in winter. The real exception to this pattern is along the coast of Alaska, where the shallow region is narrow and often contains thick multiyear ice in winter.

Some of these peripheral seas, such as Hudson Bay and the Chukchi Sea, are extremely productive and support healthy populations of marine mammals such as seals, walrus, whales – and polar bears.

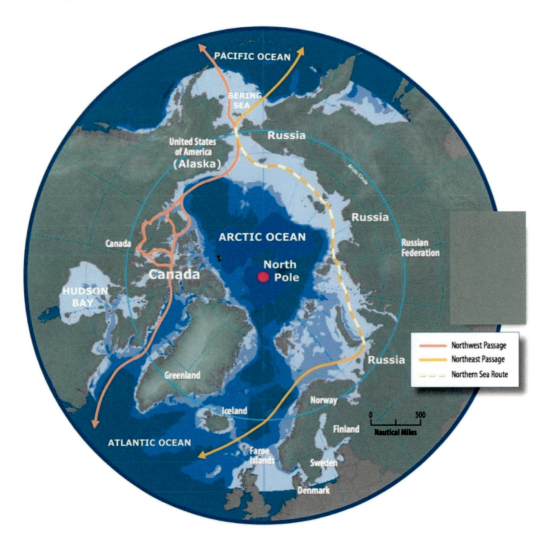

Figure 2. Polar bears live primarily in the peripheral seas of the Arctic Ocean, areas colored light blue on this map, including Hudson Bay (depths <300m). No one knows if bears live year round in the deep Arctic Basin around the North Pole (dark blue) since it has never been surveyed in winter. But single bears and family groups have been documented in the Arctic Basin from spring through fall, some of them feeding on seals.

Polar bears have been divided into 19 'subpopulations' for international management purposes by the Polar Bear Specialist Group (PBSG) of the International Union for the Conservation of Nature (IUCN) (Fig. 3). The IUCN publishes a Red List of threatened and endangered species worldwide (more on this in Ch. 4).

It is known that polar bears formerly used islands in the Bering Sea as summer refuge areas and denning sites (St. Matthew and perhaps St. Lawrence), and ranged as far south in spring as the Gulf of St. Lawrence (Fig. 3). But bear numbers were much larger then: the wholesale slaughter by whalers that took place from 1880-1930 – combined with post-WWII unregulated hunting – reduced local and global population sizes to a fraction of their former glory (see details Ch. 4). We will probably never know how many polar bears existed before that great slaughter began.

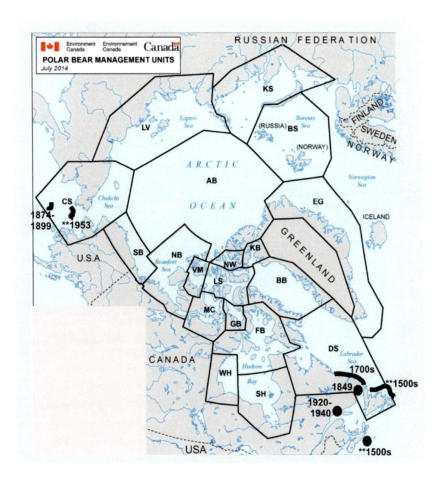

Figure 3. Polar bear management areas showing former confirmed and presumed breeding areas and historic era sightings of polar bears. Map modified from version issued by Environment Canada in 2014 (legend removed). AB, Arctic Basin; EG, East Greenland; DS, Davis Strait; BB, Baffin Bay; KB, Kane Basin; FB, Foxe Basin; SH, Southern Hudson Bay; WH, Western Hudson Bay; GB, Gulf of Boothia; MC, M'Clintock Channel; LS, Lancaster Sound; VM, Viscount Melville; NW, Norwegian Bay; NB, Northern Beaufort Sea; SB, Southern Beaufort Sea; CS, Chukchi Sea; LV, Laptev Sea; KS, Kara Sea; BS, Barents Sea.

Seasonal sea ice changes

Sea ice coverage changes from winter to summer and year to year (Figs. 4 and 5). Sea ice extent can be highly variable in different regions: for example, some years there will be more ice than average in some areas during the winter and less in others; but such changes do not always impact regions where polar bears live (Fig. 1).

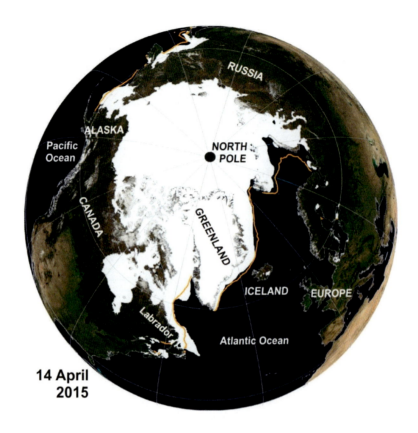

Figure 4. Some years in the spring, there is more ice than average off the coast of Labrador, Canada, and west of Greenland (as there was in 2015, shown here) while in other years, there is less.

Even at the lowest extent since 1979 (experienced in 2012, see Fig. 5), there was still an area of ice more than 3.0 mkm² remaining in the Arctic Basin in late September – that's about one and a half times the size of Greenland (Fig. 6).

Each year, newly-frozen sea ice (called first year ice) gets 6-9 feet (2-3 meters) thick over the winter, although some gets buckled and compressed into even thicker patches. First year ice is thick enough to support denning females over the winter.

Overall, first year ice that melts completely every summer is the best ice for polar bears because it's thick enough for support but is also home to Arctic seal and walrus prey.

New ice forming in the fall and melting ice in the summer needs to be only about 3-4 inches (about 10 centimeters) thick to support an adult male bear. Seals are attracted to 3-4 inch thick ice, especially in the fall, because it provides a potential resting surface for them after months with little or no ice.

Therefore, seals on or near such new fall sea ice provide important hunting opportunities for polar bears.

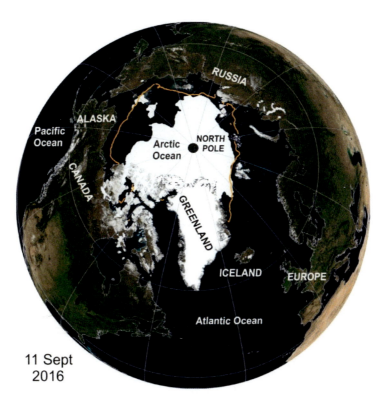

Figure 5. Sea ice near the September minimum in 2016 (11 September, minimum called on 10 September).

Figure 6. Greenland (right) covers an area of just over 2.1 mkm². If only this amount of ice ever remained in the summer sometime in the future (it has not happened yet), this would still represent an enormous area of refuge for polar bears spending the summer on the sea ice. A so-called "ice-free" Arctic would still have an area of ice covering about 1 mkm² north of Greenland and the northern Canadian Arctic islands, because the ice is so thick (15 meters or more) it could never melt completely over the short Arctic summer.

Many polar bears can, and often do, live their entire lives on the sea ice. Those are the bears you rarely hear about. In the areas surrounding the Arctic Basin (such as the Southern Beaufort or the Barents Sea), bears have the option of retreating to land, during the summer when the sea ice retreats northward, or staying with the ice. And, while researchers focus on those that come to shore, in fact *most* of the bears in those areas still remain on the ice, as they have always done. Other bears routinely spend 2-5 months on land during the summer when the first year sea ice melts completely (Fig. 7).

For those bears that spend their entire lives on the sea ice, the multiyear ice that remains in the Arctic Basin (ice greater than one year old) becomes their summer refuge.

In other words, while sea ice is required during the spring for feeding and mating, polar bears can use land in other seasons or stay on the sea ice. As I will discuss in Chapter 3, this flexibility has made it possible for the species we call polar bear (*Ursus maritimus*) to survive sea ice changes of extraordinary magnitude over several hundred thousand years.

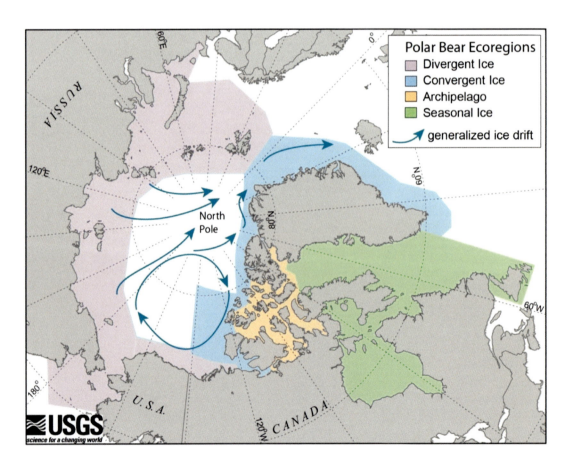

Figure 7. These are the so-called polar bear 'ecoregions' that some biologists use to characterize present and future polar bear habitat. It's useful in this context to illustrate that bears in the green areas spend 2-5 months on land during the summer because all of the first year ice melts completely, while bears in the other regions can choose to spend those 2-5 summer months on land or on the sea ice.

Where females build maternity dens

Polar bears mate in April or May but fertilized eggs do not begin to grow until fall, a biological phenomenon called 'delayed implantation.' The eggs will not develop on schedule if the female does not possess enough stored fat in the fall, so mating does not ensure a pregnancy will follow. Usually one or two cubs are born, but triplets are possible if a female is very fat.

Some females build their maternity dens on the ice and give birth there over the winter

Most females in the Chukchi and Beaufort Seas are known to spend their entire lives at sea and this may also be the case for some bears in the East Siberian and the Laptev Seas off eastern Siberia, as well as for some that live in the Canadian Arctic Archipelago.

However, bears in the Kara and Barents Seas, off western Russia and Norway, seem to den on land (since there are many islands available), as do bears in most regions of eastern North American where the ice melts each summer, as it does in Hudson Bay, and Baffin Bay (which lies between western Greenland and Baffin Island).

There is evidence from the Southern Beaufort that some pregnant females switch between denning on land and denning on sea ice. Additional evidence from the Barents Sea indicates that some pregnant females change which piece of land they use when it is time to make their maternity dens: in years with lots of sea ice they choose one of the islands in eastern Svalbard, Norway; but in years of low sea ice they choose one of the islands in Franz Josef Land, Russia.

Although this movement has not yet been confirmed, it seems the obvious explanation for the fact that Svalbard area bear numbers increased significantly between 2004 and 2015 despite several years when denning on Svalbard was impossible – if females did not switch to denning on Franz Josef Land but instead abandoned their pregnancies, the population could not have shown an increase.

The willingness to change where they make their maternity dens gives polar bear females the critical behavioral adaptability they need to survive in the Arctic, since sea ice conditions have changed enormously over geological time as well as over decades and centuries (more on this later).

Behavioral adaptability in choosing denning sites is one reflection of the fact that polar bears lack the strong territoriality typical of brown bears (aka grizzlies, their most closely related species). Being strongly territorial is not a useful way to be in an environment that can change so markedly from year to year. While some bears appear to be loyal to particular denning locations or feeding areas when conditions are relatively stable (which biologists call 'fidelity'), this does not mean that most bears will refuse to move from their preferred locations if sea ice conditions change markedly (Fig. 9).

Just because we have not had the opportunity to witness this flexibility in action does not mean it does not exist – we see the *result* of this innate adaptability in the very existence of polar bears today.

Ultimately, polar bears so loyal to particular areas for feeding or denning that they refuse to change, even if conditions demand it, are detrimental to the survival of the species: they will be selected against during times of adverse environmental change (i.e., they will die or fail to produce offspring).

Adaptable, flexible polar bear individuals – and especially females – not only survive climate change but also ensure the survival of the species over time.

Figure 8. Southern Beaufort Sea females, like this one spending some time onshore in Alaska, have been known to switch from making their dens on sea ice to land or from land to sea ice.

Chapter 2 Feasting/Fasting Life of Polar Bears

It's quite simple, really – polar bears gorge themselves on as many newborn seals as they can eat in the early spring and top up with whatever they can kill or find during the rest of the year, especially in fall. The life of feast and fast is the one they have known since they became a species adapted to the Arctic.

While polar bears also kill and consume beluga whales and narwhal trapped by ice, as well as the occasional walrus or terrestrial animal (like geese), these food sources are much less important than fat baby seals (Fig. 9). So, for polar bears, early spring is the critical period for feeding (Fig. 10).

Spring is defined as April-June above the Arctic Circle; but in more southerly areas (like Hudson Bay and Davis Strait), spring is effectively late February to the middle of May or so. Seal pups are born earlier in the south and sea ice breaks up well before it will further north.

Figure 9. Left: Ringed seals (*Phoca hispida*) are the smallest of all the Arctic seals but live virtually everywhere polar bears do. The pup shown here is a fat, newly-weaned youngster, approximately 50% fat by weight. Estimated global population size for ringed seals is almost certainly >4 million. Bearded seals (*Erignathus barbatus*), not shown here, are similarly distributed throughout the Arctic and are much larger, but there are fewer of them. Right: Harp seals (*Pagophilus groenlandicus*) are the primary prey for polar bears in the Davis Strait off eastern North America. Since the collapse of the sealing industry there, harp seal numbers have exploded. As a consequence, this single subpopulation of harp seals may now exceed the global population of ringed seals, which provides a huge prey base for Davis Strait polar bears (whose numbers, not surprisingly, have also been increasing).

Polar bear data collectors rarely, if ever, point out this difference in timing. Therefore, if sea ice breakup some year has begun in earnest in late May or June in southern regions, they might make much of the dire consequences of lost spring feeding opportunities for polar bears.

You can see that part of such a statement would be technically correct (May and June *are* considered spring months in the Arctic) but the second part is not – there are few lost hunting opportunities of the intensive variety critical to polar bears because the peak feeding period has ended naturally by that time in these southern regions.

Most seal pups are weaned by late May to early June, when they are 50% fat by weight (Fig. 9). Pups are abandoned by their mothers at this point because the adults' attention turns to mating.

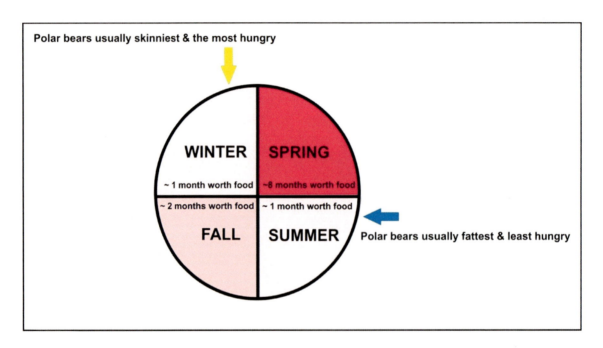

Figure 10. A graphic interpretation of approximate food intake for polar bears per season (note that times marking beginning and end of each season are generally earlier/later for bears that live south of the Arctic Circle than for bears further north). Excess spring feeding is critical for polar bears because it allows them to store fat to tide them over summer and winter periods, when food is limited or non-existent. Fall is an important top-up hunting season which allows bears to replenish fat lost during the summer fast.

Fat, newly-weaned seal pups remain on the ice for 1-3 weeks, where they are extremely vulnerable to predation by polar bears. The fatter these predator-naïve seal pups are, the better polar bears like them and fat is always eaten first. When pups are plentiful, experienced bears may eat only the fat and leave the rest for younger bears and other scavengers (such as Arctic foxes).

Within a few weeks (by mid-May to mid-June depending on the area), newly-weaned seal pups take to the water to learn how to feed themselves. Once young pups have entered the water to feed, only adults and subadults remain on the ice while they molt their hair coats. By the middle of June at the latest – when sea ice starts its annual breakup and the melt cycle begins in earnest – only wary older seals are available prey for polar bears out on the ice.

By the end of July or so, older ringed seals also take to the open water to feed over the summer, leaving only older bearded seals and a few adult harp seals available as prey for polar bears on the ice.

Figure 11. Polar bears may attempt to hunt and kill the older bearded and harp seals that are available to them on the sea ice over the summer but they are not often successful (although ringed seals are the most important prey species in the spring, they move to open water to feed over the summer and are therefore safe from polar bear predation). Some bears on the ice over the summer do not even bother trying to hunt. The bears that learn to successfully stalk and kill seals on summer ice are often the fattest bears on the ice, like this big male.

Most polar bears are fattest in the early summer

Children and adults alike are often taught that polar bears need to be fat to keep them warm over the frigid Arctic winters but that's a myth. Observations show that polar bears are almost always skinniest in late winter when it's still very cold, and heaviest in early summer after feeding all spring on fat young seals (Figs. 10 and 12).

Thick fur and shelter keep polar bears warm in winter, although some residual fat helps. Mothers emerging from dens with new cubs in early spring are often quite lean and need to find food quickly.

Figure 12. Polar bears are usually fattest in early summer (left), when Arctic cold has moderated significantly; they are leanest during the coldest part of the winter, when thick fur, shelter, and some residual fat keeps them warm. Right: Polar bear females making their maternity dens onshore may have gone eight months without food, so when these bears emerge from their dens in early spring, they are in desperate need of newborn seals to eat.

Starvation is the leading cause of death for polar bears

Young subadult polar bears hunting alone for the first time (2-5 years old) are less experienced than older bears and often less successful hunters. But young males, especially, also face the challenge of having adult males steal the kills they do make, as do past-their-prime elderly and injured bears.

As a consequence, very young and very old bears end up eating fewer seals than they need and are apt to be food-deprived by the time summer comes.

Currently, after decades of hunting bans and restrictions, there are many more older males in virtually all subpopulations than there were in the early 1970s, which means more big males around to make the lives of both subadult and elderly bears difficult. More subadult and elderly bears having trouble finding enough food in spring can mean more food-deprived bears to cause trouble onshore over the summer, including attacks on people.

Bears that have not fed sufficiently during the spring will almost certainly struggle to survive the summer fast. But the real challenge is the fast imposed by the cold and dark that descends on the Arctic in winter. Bears that have not fed sufficiently during the spring but survive through the fall invariably disappear over the winter. Pregnant females that have not stored enough fat before entering maternity dens may lose their cubs before spring, or emerge in desperate need of finding food quickly.

Chapter 3   Evolution & Climate Change

From warm interglacial periods to unimaginably cold glacial times, polar bears have survived some spectacular changes in sea ice conditions. Polar bears emerged as a new species somewhere between 400,000 and 1,200,000 years ago, but genetic evidence for their age varies and fossil evidence is scant.

To ignore this reality, as virtually all polar bear data collectors do, is to present an incomplete species story. Suggesting that less ice than we have at present is a new condition for polar bears, and an existential threat to their survival, denies the evidence that polar bears survived at least one period with much less ice than we have at present. It also glosses over how very difficult survival must have been for polar bears during severe glacial periods, when thick sea ice actually drove them out of the Arctic.

Last Glacial Maximum vs. Eemian Interglacial polar bear habitat

While the polar bear is an Ice Age species, genetic and fossil evidence suggest it barely survived the profound sea ice changes associated with the Last Glacial Maximum (LGM), one of the most severe glacial periods of the Pleistocene (about 26,000-11,500 calendar years ago). Along with tremendously thick ice sheets covering much of the Northern Hemisphere (including the Arctic Basin), sea levels were approximately 125 m (410 ft.) lower than today, which further altered the landscape.

Polar bears and Arctic seals during the LGM would have had a restricted range in the Northern Hemisphere, as shown in Fig. 13, which shows the approximate extent of perennial and annual sea ice.

There was much sea ice over the northern oceans during the LGM in areas where ice does not form today, and in the Arctic Basin the ice was so thick (perhaps 1 km) it would have excluded all the marine mammals that use it today. Much of what is now productive polar bear, ringed seal and bearded seal habitat (see Ch. 1, Fig. 2) had become dry land (e.g., the Bering Strait), or was covered by a continental ice sheet (e.g. Hudson Bay). Perennial ice in Baffin Bay, Davis Strait, and East Greenland may have been too thick to support many seals and polar bears, like the Central Canadian Arctic today.

It's not hard to see that the approximate area covered by seasonal ice during the height of the LGM would have been considerably smaller than is present now in March (Ch. 1, Fig. 1). Polar bear populations would also have been split into Atlantic and Pacific segments with no hope of any mixing.

Geneticist Charlotte Lindqvist and colleagues (2010) suggested that the extreme conditions of the last Ice Age could have led to a severe population decline that would account for the so-called "genetic bottleneck" evident in modern polar bear DNA about that time (in their study and in others). This genetic evidence suggests that sea ice conditions during the LGM had a huge impact on polar bear numbers and had a more severe effect than previous glacial periods *or* the warm conditions of previous interglacials, including the last one, which is variously called the Eemian or MIS 5e, and lasted from about 130,000-110,000 calendar years ago.

During the warm Eemian Interglacial, summer temperatures were 5-8^0 C warmer in parts of the Arctic and annual global mean temperature was about 1^0 C warmer than today. At its climax, there was no sea ice in the Bering Sea *during the winter* and virtually ice-free conditions existed in the summer (see Ch. 1, pg. 5). The Holocene Climate Maximum that followed the LGM (about 10,000-8,000 years ago) was similarly warm, but for a shorter period of time.

Yet, polar bears apparently survived the Eemian and early Holocene warm periods with only a moderate drop in population size – nothing like the scourge wrought by the LGM.

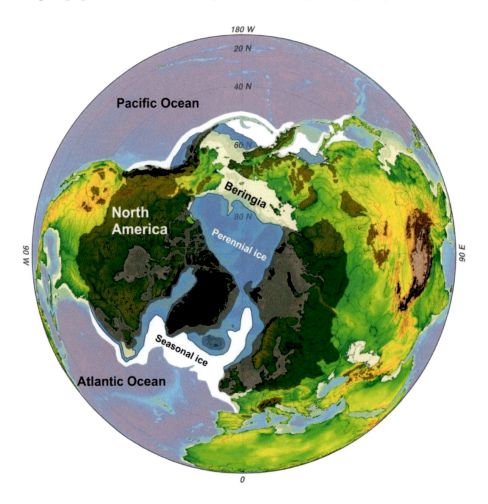

Figure 13. Approximate sea ice extent at the Last Glacial Maximum: blue is perennial sea ice (ice that is present year round) and white is seasonal sea ice at its maximum extent in late winter. Purple is open ocean; black and dark grey are continental ice sheets; cream is land exposed by lower sea level (e.g. Beringia). Only seasonal ice would have been available habitat for polar bears and Arctic seals. The sea ice additions are based on a large number of studies that document the extent of perennial sea ice and the limits of annual sea ice during the LGM. While this is an approximation only (and may change somewhat with additional research), it is a plausible picture of the sea ice habitat available to polar bears and Arctic seals at that time. Sea ice added to a standard Wikipedia image showing land-based ice sheets by US Forest Service geologist J.F. Baichtal, labels added by me.

Chapter 4   Conservation and Protection

As I mentioned in Chapter 1, during the period 1880-1930 polar bears were subjected to an appalling slaughter by commercial whalers who had killed so many Arctic whales there were virtually none left to pursue; this was followed by a period of intense unregulated hunting that lasted into the 1960s. These events combined to reduce local and global population sizes to a fraction of their former numbers.

We will never know for sure exactly how many polar bears were left by the time protective measures were put in place, a reality shared by virtually all species hunted to near extinction, such as sea otters and northern fur seals. Such numbers are acknowledged by scientists to be educated guesses.

However, based on numbers of documented kills and reduced sightings in areas where they were once abundant, the global population of polar bears was probably somewhere between 5,000 and 15,000 in 1960. Some regions were more heavily impacted by over-hunting than others, but polar bears worldwide were clearly in trouble.

Along with all large species of whales, Atlantic walrus, sea otters, and northern fur seals, wanton over-hunting had reduced polar bears to dangerously low numbers compared to historical levels. People were rightly concerned.

In 1973, the newly formed Polar Bear Specialist Group (PBSG) of the International Union for the Conservation of Nature (IUCN) helped broker an international treaty to protect polar bears by restricting hunting across the entire global range. Member nations with polar bears – Canada, Russia, USA, Norway, and Denmark (for Greenland) – appointed their leading polar bear biologists to the PBSG. The group's mandate was to initiate and coordinate polar bear research, but it was also meant to track population size.

It was not until 1988 that members of the PBSG felt they had enough biological information to suggest that polar bears were indeed 'vulnerable' to extinction (a designation similar to 'threatened'). While they gave no population size at that time, in 1981 they had estimated the global total to be 16,755 to 26,798 (calculated by me, based on the minimum and maximum estimates provided in their table).

However, by 1996, polar bear numbers had increased under hunting restrictions to about 25,000 animals. The IUCN Red List designation dropped to 'least concern' and remained there for ten years.

Polar bears had been saved.

And today they are still going strong. The last estimate, calculated in 2015 (which included all subpopulations except the Arctic Basin, assumed to have few, if any, year round residents), was 22,000-31,000 – or approximately 26,500 bears.

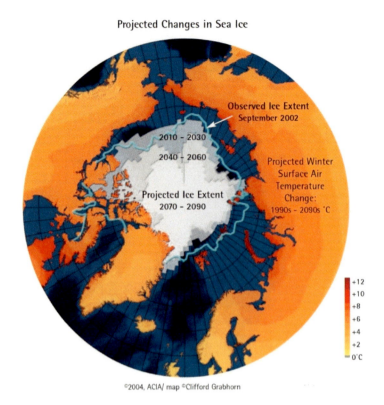

Figure 14a. Above: 'Projected' or predicted sea ice changes in 2004, used by the PBSG to conclude that polar bears were 'vulnerable' to extinction in 2006. USGS biologists used slightly different data but the general answer was the same: summer sea ice levels of about 3-5 mkm² (with some margin of error) were not expected until 2040-2060 and beyond. Compare this to the level recorded for 2012 shown in Fig. 14b below.

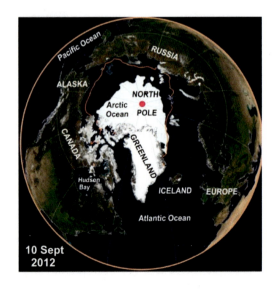

Figure 14b. Right: Documented sea ice extent near the September minimum for 2012 (shown is 10 September); Lowest extents since 1979 at the yearly minimum were in 2007 (at 18 September, 4.15 mkm²), 2012 (at 16 September, 3.39 mkm²) and 2016 (at 10 September, 4.14 mkm²) and the extent at the minimum for 2015 was 4.43 mkm². Extent figures according to the US National Snow and Ice Data Center (NSIDC).

Chapter 5 Failure of Polar Bear Predictions

The move back to 'least concern' on the IUCN Red List in 1996 did not seem to please PBSG biologists. They decided to use 'future threats' from global warming to convince the IUCN's Red List organization to move polar bears back into the 'vulnerable' category.

The predictions

A future threats strategy had never before been used for any species, and the evidence presented to support it for polar bears was weak to say the least. Based only on the opinion of the assessment writers and early-generation summer sea ice predictions (Fig. 14a, facing page), they determined with high confidence that global polar bear numbers would decline by >30% by 2050.

In 2008, US Geological Survey biologists (who were also PBSG members) used the same strategy with the US Fish & Wildlife Service to get polar bears listed as 'threatened' under the Endangered Species Act (ESA) – they assessed not just polar bears managed by the US, but the entire global population, using sea ice models developed for the 2007 IPCC report (IPCC AR4).

The USGS developed polar bear survival models that were based on one biologist's opinion of how polar bears would respond to projected summer sea ice changes, because winter and spring sea ice were not expected to change much over the next 95 years (i.e., loss of summer ice was the only habitat change considered to be a potential risk to health or survival). These experts predicted confidently that by 2050, bears in 10 vulnerable subpopulations would be extirpated (reduced to zero) and that the global population would be reduced by two thirds (Fig. 15).

This meant the 20,000-25,000 polar bears living in 2005 were anticipated to drop to only 6,660-8,325 in direct response to the sea ice coverage in summer expected in 45 years. **No bears – none at all – were expected to continue living in Hudson Bay, west of Greenland or anywhere in Russia or the US by the middle of the 21st century.**

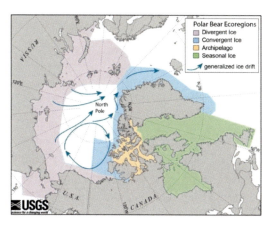

Figure 15. American researchers from the US Geological Survey amassed the evidence used to justify listing polar bears as 'threatened' under the Endangered Species Act in a series of internal government reports. They predicted that by 2050 (within 3 polar bear generations), polar bears would no longer exist in the areas colored light green and purple in this map – i.e., 10 subpopulations (out of 19 total) were predicted to be extirpated by 2050, bringing the global population down to 6,660-8,325 (from 20,000-25,000 in 2005). See a larger version of this map in Ch. 1.

The observations

Now that a decade or so has passed, the problem with these confident predictions of impending catastrophe are apparent. Sea ice in summer has declined much more than expected since 2006. In fact, starting in 2007 (even before the US Fish & Wildlife could officially proclaim polar bears to be 'threatened' with extinction), summer sea ice has reached levels not anticipated until 2050 at the earliest (Fig. 14a, b) or about 3-5 mkm^2 (give or take some measuring error).

The dreaded sea ice decline of 2050 had come almost 45 years early – but by 2015, polar bears had experienced potentially devastating summer ice levels for almost 10 years straight.

Unfortunately, none of the figures or graphs used in publications promoting the predictions made by USGS biologists for 2050 were of high enough resolution to reproduce here (e.g., Amstrup et al. 2008, Plate 8) but they show quite clearly that September ice extents expected at mid-century by USGS were very similar to those calculated by earlier ice prediction models shown in Figure 14a.

Specifically, the Amstrup figure (not shown here) illustrates that the seasonal minimum ice extent observed in 2007 (marked on the figure as 4.13 mkm^2 but now officially 4.15 mkm^2, according to NSIDC), which corresponded to an area of 3.5 mkm^2 of 'preferred polar bear habitat' (ice of 50% concentration over continental shelves), was lower than five out of ten model projections for September 2050 (i.e., 2045-2055). The other five predictions were much lower than observed.

In other words, the sea ice that polar bears got in the summer of 2007 was much lower than the five best guesses ice experts and USGS biologists predicted they would have in 2050.

So, what happened? Was the Arctic littered with bear carcasses? Were polar bears wildly eating each other in their desperation to survive? Did deaths by drowning escalate to unfathomable numbers?

Actually, not much of anything disastrous happened. But you wouldn't have known this by listening to the polar bear data collectors and their future-survival computer modeling colleagues. With very few exceptions, they said nothing of the catastrophe that did not happen and still speak of the dire prospects of declining ice as if the worst they imagined back in 2006 hadn't already occurred.

Since then, continued research has found that bears in the Chukchi Sea (Fig. 16) – considered one of the most vulnerable of all subpopulations – are thriving. Chukchi bears were in better shape (in terms of body condition and number of cubs produced) after 2007 than they had been in the 1980s, when they had a much shorter open water period in summer. It turns out that a longer open water season meant ringed seals could feed longer (which is almost certainly true for ringed seals worldwide); the seals produced more fat pups the following spring, which meant polar bears had more to eat.

In other words, the data strongly support a conclusion that less summer ice is actually *better* for Chukchi bears, not worse.

Finally, more bears in the Chukchi and Southern Beaufort Seas have been found to be spending longer periods of time on land in the summer from 2007 onward than they did in the 1980s but no adverse effects on reproduction or survival have been documented, substantiating other studies that show polar bears eat little during the summer whether they are on the ice or on land.

Some other life history assumptions made by data collectors also turned out to be wrong. For example, while biologists formerly concluded (from studies in the 1980s) that polar bears preferred only sea ice of 50% concentration or greater, it now appears the bears are quite capable of utilizing ice at concentrations so low they are not recorded by routine satellite imagery (i.e., <15% concentration). Cannibalism did not increase dramatically with less ice, as predicted, nor did deaths by drowning or incidents of hybridization with brown bears (also known as grizzly bears).

Figure 16. A fat and healthy Chukchi Sea polar bear female and her chubby cub. During a recent study done in 2008-2011 (i.e., just after the first extended open water season of 2007), several females with triplet litters were documented (a phenomenon rarely, *if ever*, recorded outside Western Hudson Bay). Several adult males weighed >100 kg more than average and were in similar body condition to bears in the stable subpopulation of Foxe Basin, which has been counted repeatedly, suggesting that despite the fact that Chukchi Sea bears have never been counted, they are also likely to be a stable subpopulation.

In addition – again contrary to predictions – the number of polar bears in the Svalbard area north of Norway, surveyed in August 2015, was found to be *up 42%* since they were last counted in 2004, despite "poor" sea ice conditions for most of that time. Although not yet confirmed, based on this result and previous research showing how much these bears move around, it seems certain that Svalbard area pregnant females shift to the archipelago of Franz Josef Land, Russia (Fig. 17) when there is not enough sea ice in the fall for them to reach preferred denning sites in eastern Svalbard (e.g. 2012 and 2013). Even in recent years (2016 included), Franz Josef Land has had surrounding ice in the fall, making this an excellent alternative option for pregnant Svalbard females, who can shift back to their preferred sites when the ice allows (as it did in the fall of 2014, just before the 2015 survey).

Polar bear numbers in Southern Hudson Bay, Western Hudson Bay, and Foxe Basin – also considered highly vulnerable – were found to have been stable since at least 2001. Davis Strait bears were also doing well – like Chukchi Sea bears, they may have had less ice in summer but they have had an abundance of seals to eat in spring (in this case, harp seals) and as a consequence, were thriving. In 2013, for the first time, Russian researchers were able to survey the Kara Sea subpopulation region (which lies just east of the Barents Sea, Fig. 17), and found about 3,200 polar bears (2,700-3,500) – which added a count for a region never before included in global population estimates.

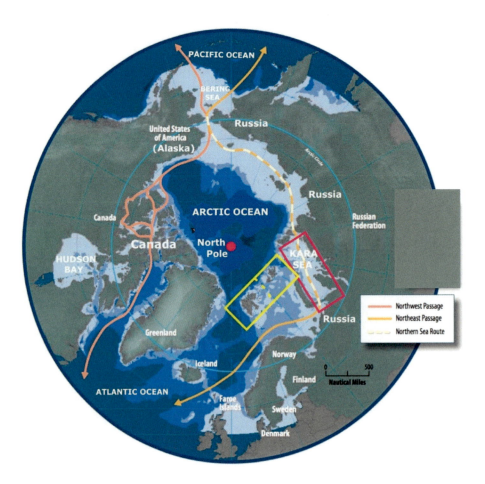

Figure 17. Location of the Kara Sea (magenta rectangle), in Western Russia, where a 2013 polar bear population size survey generated an estimate of 2,700-3,500 (about 3,200). Prior to 2015, no polar bears from this region were included in any global totals. Also marked is the Barents Sea (yellow rectangle); a dashed line separates the two major archipelagos used by polar bear females for denning (Svalbard, Norway and Franz Josef Land, Russia).

Oddly, none of the data collectors or modelers have expressed surprise that year after year of summer sea ice, the likes of which they did not expect until mid-century, did not cause a massive decline in polar bear numbers (Fig. 14b): in 2005, there were 20,000-25,000 bears (about 22,500 with some areas not counted) but by 2015, there were 22,000-31,000 bears (about 26,500 with all areas counted). Furthermore, studies completed or data published since July 2015 increased the unofficial total to about 28,500 (see Crockford 2017). This suggests a growing global population, because subpopulations that have not been closely monitored (such as East Greenland) may have grown just as much as studied ones have done.

A statistical analysis is not required to see that the future survival models for polar bears were wrong – a 67% decline in population size did not happen and polar bears did not struggle to survive despite experiencing supposedly 'deadly' levels of summer sea ice virtually every year since 2007.

Chapter 6   The Biggest Threat to Polar Bears

Lack of abundant fat seals to eat in spring is the single greatest threat to polar bear health and survival, over both short and long time scales, no matter what is happening with summer sea ice.

It is apparent that the biggest threat to modern polar bear populations is the same one that has threatened polar bear survival since they became a distinct species – not enough fat newborn seals to eat in the spring. This is the premise of my science-based novel about polar bears (*EATEN*), in which southern Davis Strait polar bears off Newfoundland and Labrador experience just such a challenge.

One phenomenon that routinely threatens the seal prey supply is thicker than usual first year ice in the spring (this was almost certainly the biggest hurdle that polar bears faced as the LGM (Ch. 2) approached its climax, as first year ice in winter became thicker year after year and expanded the sea ice beyond the Arctic proper). Variable snow cover over sea ice is another factor.

Neither of these phenomena has been included in models of future polar bear survival – only the loss of summer sea ice has been included as a risk factor. Thus, any decline in polar bear condition, survival, or cub production is assumed to be the result of reduced summer ice because polar bear numbers are assumed not to vary at all due to natural conditions, over short *or* long time periods.

In my opinion, this disregard of well-known risk factors presented by variable spring conditions is particularly disingenuous. But read through the evidence below and decide for yourself.

Effects of variable ice thickness on ringed seals and polar bears

Ultimately, the reason that thick ice and variable snow cover are problems for polar bears is that they are problems for seals – especially ringed seals.

Ringed seals are unique among all Arctic seal species, in that they maintain breathing holes in the sea ice over the winter and spring – other species live at the edge of the pack ice or in so-called 'polynyas' (areas of sea ice where currents maintain open water for all or part of the winter and spring). Arctic water is warmer than air during the winter, so seals usually stay off the ice. But they all need access to air every few minutes so they can breathe – if they get caught under ice without access to open water, they will die of suffocation. This has been recorded often for small Arctic whales but rarely for seals.

Female ringed seals are also unique in that they usually construct a snow cave on top of the ice (called a lair, see Fig. 18) in which they give birth to their pups and nurse them until weaning – other species give birth in the open, on the exposed surface of the ice.

If the first year ice on which a ringed seal female has constructed her birth lair becomes more than about 6 ft. thick (2 m.) during the nursing period, she will not be able to get out of the water to attend her pup and must abandon it. Similarly, a ringed seal female might find that the first year ice in the area in which she would normally give birth (such as a shallow water area close to shore) has become too thick for her purposes by late winter and she must look elsewhere for a suitable location.

Under either circumstance, a large mortality event of seal pups or a massive redistribution of pregnant seals relative to shore ensues which can have deadly consequences for polar bears.

If a number of polar bear females have made their winter maternity dens near areas habitually used by pregnant ringed seals in a year when one of these periodic ice thickening events occurs, the hapless bears may emerge in spring with their cubs only to discover no source of food. The thick near-shore ice means no (or few) newborn ringed seals are available close to shore for new mothers to prey upon.

These unlucky female polar bears will probably lose their cubs to starvation and may starve themselves (either immediately or months later). Lack of abundant seal pups close to shore also makes life difficult for mothers with older cubs – because they are hunting for two or three – as well as for subadult bears hunting on their own for the first time. Many of these vulnerable individuals will enter the summer fasting season without enough fat and will later die of starvation over the fall or winter.

We are talking about the deaths of tens of dozens of bears, not just a few. Hundreds more bears may simply leave the impacted region for areas of thinner ice, which to field biologists counting bears for a population assessment looks the same as bears that have died.

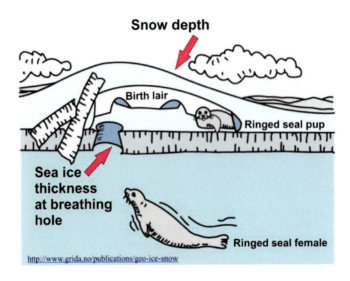

Figure 18. This useful diagram shows how and why ringed seals are uniquely vulnerable to variations in snow depth and ice thickness. If the ice gets much more than about 6 ft. thick (2 m), females cannot maintain either the breathing holes for themselves or the access tunnels into the birth lairs they build for their pups. If the covering snow melts prematurely in early spring (documented to have happened only once, in April 1979, but may have occurred at other times without our knowledge), the pup may die of exposure or become an easy polar bear meal. If the snow covering the lair becomes very thick, polar bears will have trouble locating birth lairs and their vulnerable pups – survival of seals improve but polar bears may starve.

There is abundant evidence that a catastrophic mortality event of this kind has occurred in the Southern Beaufort polar bear subpopulation every 10 years or so since the 1960s – in other words, ever since seal and polar bear populations have been tracked routinely in this region.

The most well-documented thick ice event for Southern Beaufort bears occurred in 1974-1976, when the population dropped by almost 50%. A catastrophic event of virtually identical magnitude (according to the researchers who witnessed both) occurred in 2004-2006, when again the population declined by about 50%. Less profoundly devastating events occurred in the early 1960s, the mid-1980s and the early 1990s (if another event has occurred since 2006, it has not been reported).

Veteran polar bear biologist Ian Stirling (2002:68) had this to say about the reduced survival of polar bears due thick spring ice in the Beaufort Sea in the mid-1970s:

> "In the eastern Beaufort Sea, in years during and following heavy ice conditions in spring, we found a marked reduction in production of ringed seal pups and consequently in the natality [cub survival] of polar bears. The effect appeared to last for about three years, after which productivity of both seals and bears increased again. These clear and major reductions in productivity of ringed seals in relation to ice conditions occurred at decadal scale intervals in the mid-1970s and 1980s and, on the basis of less complete data, probably in the mid-1960s as well."

And as noted above, an event as severe as the mid-1970s also occurred in the mid-2000s.

A little-known but critical fact is that a population survey by US Geological Survey (USGS) biologists was conducted over that 2004-2006 period and formed the basis of the justification for the US Fish and Wildlife Service to list polar bears as 'threatened' with extinction under the Endangered Species Act (ESA) due to sea ice loss.

The internal USGS reports did not mention the paucity of ringed seal pups and the thick ice conditions of 2004-2006 in the eastern Beaufort that their Canadian colleagues found during the 2004 and 2005 spring field seasons, even though Canadian Ian Stirling was a co-author on one of the USGS reports. While USGS biologists *did* note incidents of winter/spring starvation and poor survival in the Southern Beaufort over the 2004-2006 period, they implied these were effects of reduced summer ice.

Official accounts of those devastating years for Southern Beaufort seals and polar bears in 2004-2006 were not published until after the US Fish and Wildlife Service ESA listing process was complete. And while a follow-up population count for 2001-2010 noted that the thick spring ice phenomenon of the mid-2000s was similar in scope, magnitude and effect as the devastating 1974-1976 event, it still presented the calculated population decline as a likely result of summer sea ice loss.

Overall, the failure of USGS future survival modelers to take into account the well-documented negative effects of these periodic thick spring ice phenomena on Southern Beaufort polar bear health and survival means that neither the statistically insignificant population decline recorded by the USGS team in 2005, nor the 25-50% decline calculated later (over 2001-2010), can be reliably attributed to the effects of reduced summer sea ice.

There was indeed a population decline in 2004-2006 in the Southern Beaufort and there was also a decline in summer sea ice in 2004 and 2005 relative to 1980s sea ice – but in this case the correlations between the two were a coincidence and scientifically false. By failing to take into account details of the natural thick spring ice phenomenon unique to this region and its known negative effect on population size, USGS modelers created useless mathematical predictions.

The reason that this phenomenon is so prominent in Southern Beaufort polar bear history, but virtually absent in others, is that this region has a distinctive geography – it is uniquely situated for developing very thick first year ice via compression against the shoreline. As Fig. 19 shows, the clockwise rotating Beaufort Gyre drives dense multiyear pack ice, which accumulates north of the Canadian Arctic Archipelago, against the land-locked first year ice that develops close to shore (called *shore-fast ice*) along Alaska and western Canada in early winter, creating deep pressure ridges (Fig. 20).

In contrast, prevailing currents in the rest of the Arctic are largely offshore or parallel to shore, so such thick ice conditions rarely develop close to shore elsewhere. However, winds can occasionally drive ice onshore in any location, leading to the development of similar-looking pressure ridges.

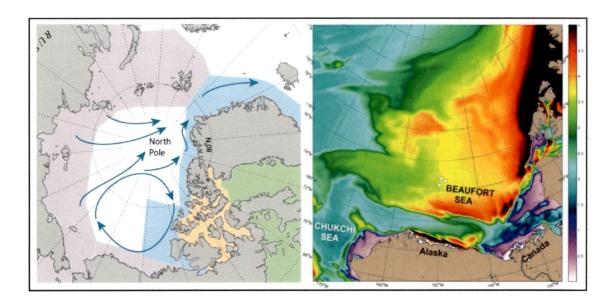

Figure 19. Left: Prevailing currents in the Arctic Basin, showing the clockwise rotation of the strong Beaufort Gyre current that drives multiyear ice from the central basin towards the exposed shores of Alaska and western Canada where shore-fast ice dominates. Most (but not all) ringed seals prefer shore-fast ice for giving birth but this preference in the Southern Beaufort puts them at risk for the occasional development of thickened compressed ice that is incompatible with the birthing process. Cropped from the USGS map shown in Ch. 1 Fig. 7. Right: Ice thickness measured and forecasted by the US Naval Research Laboratory (HYCOM Consortium) on 18 April 2015, when ice 4-5 meters thick developed along the central Alaskan shoreline (band of black and red) and more thick, multiyear ice was being pressed ashore by the Beaufort Gyre.

Figure 20. Beaufort Sea pressure ridges in spring 1949.

Effects of variable snow cover and ice thickness on ringed seals and polar bears

Deep snow over the birthing lairs of ringed seals (Fig. 18 and 21) means pups are well protected from polar bear predation – the seals do well but the polar bears do not. For example, deep snow over ice was suspected to have negatively impacted the body condition of Western Hudson Bay polar bears in 1983. That fall, Churchill had a spike in problem bears, cub survival was lower than average, and bears in poor condition were common in the fall. Freeze-up was much later than average that year (as it was in 2016) but the fact that bears came ashore in poor condition in 1983 suggests that the survival problems they had later in the year were primarily the result of poor spring feeding conditions.

This conclusion is corroborated by the fact that in 1983, ringed seal researchers working in Western Hudson Bay reported high mean snow depths in April-May (>50 cm). Onshore measurements had to be used as a proxy for on-ice snow depth, since there are no data for snow depth over sea ice on Hudson Bay. Polar bear and ringed seal researchers agree that snow deeper than about 30 cm leads to poor hunting success for polar bears but good survival for seals. Deep snow in spring might be good news for ringed seals but it's usually bad news for polar bears (Fig. 22).

In contrast, shallow snow cover over birthing lairs (considered to be less than 25-32 cm over the lair, or less than 20 cm over flat ice), can mean the snow caves are easier for polar bears to break into – this is good news for polar bears but bad news for ringed seals. Mean snow depth was reportedly at or below the critical 20 cm threshold in April-May in Western Hudson Bay once in the 1960s and eight times between 1993 and 2000.

There is an added risk for ringed seal snow caves with little snow cover – they can collapse if there is a warm spell (made worse by rain), although this can occur when snow depth is average or even above average. Lair collapse (or snow made soft by spring rain) leaves pups especially vulnerable to predation, but so far, this phenomenon has been documented only once: off the coast of southeastern Baffin Island in April 1979.

Figure 21. Snow over sea ice provides shelter for bears as well as for ringed seal pups.

Figure 22. Female polar bear with new cub of the year on spring sea ice.

Chapter 7 Summary

- Total polar bear habitat in winter has been fairly consistent at about 14.0 mkm² (1979-2016).
- Polar bears live primarily in the shallow peripheral seas of the Arctic, including Hudson Bay.
- There has been no contraction of polar bear range due to recent sea ice loss.
- Overall, first year ice is the best habitat for polar bears – it suits all of their needs.
- Polar bears hunt Arctic seals (and sometimes, small whales) from the surface of the sea ice.
- Many polar bears live their entire lives at sea but some spend 2-5 months on land from summer through fall.
- Some pregnant females den on the ice, some den on land and some switch from one to the other depending on conditions – of all polar bears, pregnant females most need to be flexible.
- Pregnant females that den on land may go more than eight months without food by the time they emerge with three month-old cubs in spring – stored fat sustains them through that time.
- Spring is the most important feeding season for polar bears – 2/3 of their food for the year is consumed in the two-three months after the first Arctic seals are born (dates vary by location).
- Most polar bears are fattest at the beginning of summer and leanest at the end of winter.
- Spring comes earlier south of the Arctic Circle than it does to the north – and it ends sooner.
- Newborn seals leave the ice soon after being weaned, which means only adult and subadult seals are potential polar bear prey from about mid-May to mid-June depending on the area.
- Adult and subadult ringed seals leave the ice in July to feed in open water, so only bearded seals and a few harp seals remain as prey for polar bears that stay on the sea ice in summer.
- Older seals are much harder for polar bears to catch and the hunts get harder as ice melt progresses in summer – wary older seals have many escape routes through the fractured ice.
- Most bears eat little over the summer, whether they are on land or on the ice.
- Every year, the leading natural cause of death for all polar bears is starvation; due to competition for seals on the ice, young and elderly bears are always at risk.
- Polar bears barely survived the effects of expanded sea ice during the last cold *Glacial* period (LGM, 26 - 11.5 thousand years ago) but the last warm *Interglacial* (Eemian, 130-110 thousand years ago) and the warm Holocene Climatic Optimum that following the LGM had a much smaller impact – much more ice appears to have been harder on polar bears than less ice.
- Polar bears were deemed 'vulnerable' to extinction by the IUCN Red List in 1988 due to over-hunting but this changed to 'Least concern' in 1996 after international protection protocols resulted in strong population growth, which was the expected result.
- In 2006, with a population estimate of 20,000-25,000, polar bear specialists insisted that future loss of sea ice due to human-caused CO^2 emissions was an imminent threat to polar bear

- survival – by 2008, the IUCN Red List predicted a population decline of >30% and USGS biologists predicted a 67% decline (and the total demise of 10 vulnerable subpopulations).
- Unfortunately, in 2007 sea ice extent in summer dropped to levels not expected until 2050 or later – future conditions assumed to be deadly to polar bears was their new reality by 2007.
- Contrary to predictions, the global polar bear population did not drop by 2/3, nor have 10 subpopulations been extirpated – in 2015, the global polar bear population size was estimated at 22,000-31,000 (about 26,500) **& data published recently bring the total to about 28,500**.
- Contrary to predictions, several so-called vulnerable subpopulations have shown positive effects of less summer ice: more open water in summer has been beneficial to bears because it is beneficial to seals (especially ringed seals).
- Recent studies also corroborate earlier ones that determined polar bears eat little during the summer whether they are on land or on the ice.
- Polar bear experts were wrong in declaring that declines in summer sea ice would mean sharp declines in polar bear numbers.
- Polar bear experts were wrong in their claims that cannibalism incidents would increase dramatically with low summer ice, that massive mortality events from drowning would occur, and that incidents of hybridization with brown/grizzly bears would increase.
- It has been confirmed that many bears move across the arbitrary subpopulation boundaries established by the IUCN Polar Bear Specialist Group, especially in the Beaufort/Chukchi Sea region and the Davis Strait/Hudson Bay region, but also *within* the Barents Sea, a practice that reflects polar bears' adaptability in the face of locally-changing ice conditions.
- In addition, polar bears have recently been found to routinely use low concentration sea ice (<15%) even though data collectors assumed they would abandon ice that dropped to <50%.
- Overall, recent research has shown that polar bear data collectors and future survival computer modelers were quite wrong a decade ago to insist that summer sea ice is essential to polar bear health; but they have so far refused to admit this – instead, they have constructed new models based on similar assumptions (e.g., summer sea ice is critical habitat) that generate similar outputs, and vigorously defend this approach.
- In addition, the modelers made a critical scientific error in glossing over data collected by their colleagues (well documented in the scientific literature), which indicates the greatest threat to polar bears is a reduction in the abundance or availability of fat baby seals to eat in the spring.
- Polar bear numbers have been known to decline by half within a single year due to sporadic failed seal pup production because of thick spring ice or heavy snow cover over ice - both ringed seal and polar bear populations can fluctuate widely due to natural causes.
- Future polar bear survival models assume such natural population size changes do not occur.
- The last two population counts undertaken for the Southern Beaufort subpopulation included a period when a devastating natural population decline occurred due to thick spring ice – ironically, this was the only subpopulation with a significant decline documented since 2004.
- Not only did US government biologists not mention the fact that a thick spring ice event occurred in the middle of their last polar bear counts, they implied that the population decline they detected was caused by sea ice loss in summer – a particularly disingenuous conclusion.

Chapter 8   Conclusions

Data amassed over the last 50 years or so on polar bear ecology, fossil history, population health, and evolution confirm that *Ursus maritimus* is a remarkable survivor of climate change.

Polar bears have survived long periods of much more ice than we have now as well as periods of much less ice, but those times of much more ice seem to have been the most devastating.

Research since 2007, in particular, has shown that polar bears are not dependent on sea ice over the summer – whether there is less ice in summer than usual makes little difference to their survival.

What makes the greatest difference to polar bear survival is variation in abundance and availability of young seal pups in early spring. A well-fed bear with plenty of stored fat at the end of spring can withstand the coming fasts of summer and winter, while a lean bear at the end of spring will likely die.

Polar bear numbers worldwide have remained stable since 2005; those studied subpopulations once considered vulnerable to the effects of low summer sea ice have all been stable or increased in size, except for one which declined due to thick spring ice conditions.

Despite this spectacular success through nine years worth of sea ice not expected until mid-century, in 2015 American government and IUCN Polar Bear Specialist Group biologists were still insisting that summer sea ice is critical for polar bear health and survival. In 2016, they became adamant that if the Arctic becomes nearly ice-free in summer, polar bears face extinction.

These experts have resolutely refused to admit they were wrong about the resilience of polar bears. Faced with data that absolutely contradicts their assumptions and predictions, they are sticking to the same 'polar bears are doomed' message they developed back in 2005/2006, using models based on the same failed assumption about the importance of summer ice. It is unclear why they won't move on.

I can only suggest it must be harder than I realized to let go of a cherished concept, especially one that has garnered grant funds essential for continued Arctic research. As a scientist who has always embraced new topics, I am baffled by this conundrum. But I am also deeply disturbed that children are still being given the impression (by the actions and words of these specialists) that so few polar bears exist today that we must breed them in zoos to assure their future survival, which is clearly nonsense.

It's as if it is the polar bear *specialist* that lacks the necessary resilience to survive through changing conditions, not the polar bear itself.

One thing I learned through my research is that the USA (via biologists at the US Geological Survey and US Fish and Wildlife Service) has been uniquely assertive amongst Arctic nations in assigning 'threatened' status to other Arctic species based on the same assumptions and criteria used to list polar bears (including bearded, ringed, and spotted seals, as well as Pacific walrus): in contrast, most other countries, as well as the IUCN Red List, list these Arctic seals and Pacific walrus as either being of 'least concern' or have not assessed them at all.

This disparity in conservation status of Arctic species should be a red flag that tells us something odd is going on with this issue. It means relatively few specialists are convinced that loss of summer sea ice is, or will be, an existential threat to the survival of Arctic-adapted marine mammals.

Let me be very clear about one thing: if in the future, sea ice concentration declined in early spring (i.e., April) for any reason, including the effects of human fossil fuel use, polar bears in some areas would definitely face large-scale mortality due to reduced prey abundance or access to prey.

For example, if breakup occurred in April in Hudson Bay, ringed seals would lose their pups before weaning and most polar bears would lose their cubs; bears that did not move north immediately to find food would die. That said, the documented responses of ringed seals and polar bears to adverse spring ice in the Southern Beaufort (as well as the survival of both species over millennia worldwide) suggest that most survivors would indeed move immediately in search of more suitable conditions.

This means local 'extirpation' of polar bear subpopulations under a hypothetical spring sea ice decline would come from emigration, not extermination – and the global population might not actually drop by very much over the long term, since the bears (and seals) might thrive in their new locations.

However, no such decline in early spring sea ice has taken place and there is no indication that it is imminent, even on a less extreme scale than the hypothetical case described above. Virtually all declines in ice extent in winter or spring so far have been in regions where polar bears do not live (Ch. 1, Fig. 1). All sea ice models – even the new ones – predict relatively small declines in winter and spring ice through to the end of the 21st century.

In other words, there is no demonstrable threat to polar bears or their prey species from some generalized decline in sea ice and that's because all significant declines so far have been in summer, which is a pattern expected to continue. Recent research from a few regions thought to be especially vulnerable to loss of summer ice has shown that polar bears and ringed seals are not merely adapting to this lower ice regime, they are thriving.

I suggest that if it was previously acceptable for polar bear specialists to use 'bad news' data from a few subpopulations as 'stand-ins' for others of a similar type in order to predict a dire future outcome for all, then it is equally acceptable today to use 'good news' data from the Chukchi Sea and Svalbard, as well as from Foxe Basin and Davis Strait, to suggest a positive future outcome for all.

Polar bear populations worldwide are currently healthy and there exists no compelling evidence that further loss of summer sea ice will drive them to the brink of extinction by 2050 or even 2100. This is the good news people need to hear, including children. Polar bears are outstanding survivors of climate change and deserve our admiration for their amazing resilience.

The existence of polar bears today is evidence of this fact. Polar bears are not misplaced brown bears eking out an existence on the frozen surface of the ocean – they are a species fine-tuned to survive (and thrive) within the constantly changing environment that is the Arctic. Polar bears will be OK.

###~###

References by page number & topic

Pg. 1-3. Where polar bears live (and other basics)

Amstrup, S.C. 2003. Polar bear (*Ursus maritimus*). In *Wild Mammals of North America*, G.A. Feldhamer, B.C. Thompson and J.A. Chapman (eds), pg. 587-610. Johns Hopkins University Press, Baltimore.

Cronin, M.A., Amstrup, S.C., et al. 2009. Genetic variation, relatedness, and effective population size of polar bears (*Ursus maritimus*) in the southern Beaufort Sea, Alaska. *Journal of Heredity* **100**: 681-690.

Derocher, A.E., Andersen, M., et al. 2010. Sexual dimorphism and the mating ecology of polar bears (*Ursus maritimus*) at Svalbard. *Behavioral Ecology and Sociobiology* **64**: 939-946.

Derocher, A.E. & Lynch, W. 2012. *Polar Bears: A Complete Guide to their Biology and Behavior.* Johns Hopkins U. Press.

De Veer, Gerrit. 1609. *The Three Voyages of William Barentsz to the Arctic Regions* (English translation). Online.

Durner, G.M. & Amstrup, S.C. 1995. Movements of a polar bear from northern Alaska to northern Greenland. *Arctic* **48**: 338-341.

Durner, G.M., Douglas, D.C., et al. 2006. A model for autumn pelagic distribution of female polar bears in the Chukchi Sea, 1987-1994. US Geological Survey. Reston, Virginia.

Crockford, S.J. 2012. *Annotated Map of Ancient Polar Bear Remains of the World.* Electronic resource available at https://polarbearscience/references ISBN 978-0-9917966-0-1.

Elliott, H.W. 1875. Polar bears on St. Matthew Island. *Harper's Weekly Journal of Civilization.* **May 1 issue.** Harper and Brothers, New York.

Elliott, H.W. & Coues, E. 1875. A report upon the condition of affairs in the territory of Alaska. US Government Printing Office, Washington. http://tinyurl.com/a8zk6yk

Ogilvie, A.E.J., Barlow, L.K. et al. 2000. North Atlantic climate c. AD 1000: Millennial reflections on the Viking discoveries of Iceland, Greenland and North America. *Weather* **55**: 34-45.

Lydersen, C. & Gjertz, I. 1986. Studies of the ringed seal (*Phoca hispida* Schreber 1775) in its breeding habitat in Kongsfjorden, Svalbard. *Polar Research* **4**: 57-63.

Packard, A.S. 1886. The former southern limits of the white or polar bear. *American Naturalist* **20(7)**: 655–659.

Peacock, E., Taylor, M.K., et al. 2013. Population ecology of polar bears in Davis Strait, Canada and Greenland. *Journal of Wildlife Management* **77**: 463–476.

Ramsay, M.A. & Stirling, I. 1988. Reproductive biology and ecology of female polar bears (*Ursus maritimus*). *Journal of Zoology London* **214**: 601-624.

Rausch, R.L. 1953. On the land mammals of St. Lawrence Island, Alaska. *Murrelet* **34**: 18–26.

Rode, K.D., Regehr, E.V., et al. 2014. Variation in the response of an Arctic top predator experiencing habitat loss: feeding and reproductive ecology of two polar bear populations. *Global Change Biology* **20**: 76-88.

Stirling, I. 2002. Polar bears and seals in the eastern Beaufort Sea and Amundsen Gulf: a synthesis of population trends and ecological relationships over three decades. *Arctic* **55 (Suppl. 1)**: 59-76.

Stirling, I. 2011. *Polar Bears: The Natural History of a Threatened Species.* Fitzhenry & Whiteside, Markham.

Stirling & Kiliaan. 1980. Population ecology studies of the polar bear in northern Labrador. Canadian Wildlife Service Occasional Paper No. 42.

Smith, P., Stirling, I., et al. 1975. Notes on the present status of the polar bear (*Ursus maritimus*) in Ungava Bay and northern Labrador. Canadian Wildlife Service, Progress Notes 53.

Van Meurs, R. & Splettstoesser, J.F. 2003. Farthest North Polar Bear (Letter to the Editor). *Arctic* **56**: 309.

Wiig, Ø., Amstrup, S., et al. 2015. *Ursus maritimus*. The IUCN Red List of Threatened Species 2015: e.T22823A14871490.

Pg. 4-6. Seasonal sea ice changes (and use by polar bears)

Arrigo, K.R. & van Dijken, G.L. 2015. Continued increases in Arctic Ocean primary production. *Progress in Oceanography* **136**: 60–70.

Brown, Z.W., van Dijken, G.L. et al. 2011. A reassessment of primary production and environmental change in the Bering Sea. *Journal of Geophysical Research* **116**: C08014. doi:10.1029/2010JC006766.

Cherry, S.G., Derocher, A.E., et al. 2013. Migration phenology and seasonal fidelity of an Arctic marine predator in relation to sea ice dynamics. *Journal of Animal Ecology* **82**: 912-921.

Derocher, A.E. 2005. Population ecology of polar bears at Svalbard, Norway. *Population Ecology* **47**: 267-275

Derocher, A.E., Andersen, M., et al. 2010. Sexual dimorphism and the mating ecology of polar bears (*Ursus maritimus*) at Svalbard. *Behavioral Ecology and Sociobiology* **64**: 939-946.

Derocher, A.E., Lunn, N.J., et al. 2004. Polar bears in a warming climate. *Integrative and Comparative Biology* **44**: 163–176.

Frey, K.E., Moore, G.W.K., et al. 2015. Divergent patterns of recent sea ice cover across the Bering, Chukchi, and Beaufort seas of the Pacific Arctic Region. *Progress in Oceanography* **136**: 32–49.

Furevik, T., Drange, H. et al. 2002. Anticipated changes in the Nordic Seas marine climate: Scenarios for 2020, 2050, and 2080. *Fisken og Havet* **2002-4**: 1-13.

Gagnon, A.S. & Gough, W.A. 2005. Trends in the dates of ice freeze-up and breakup over Hudson Bay, Canada. *Arctic* **58**: 370-382.

George, J.C., Druckenmiller, M.L., et al. 2015. Bowhead whale body condition and links to summer sea ice and upwelling in the Beaufort Sea. *Progress in Oceanography* **136**: 250-262.

Meier, W.N., Hovelsrud, G.K., et al. 2014. Arctic sea ice in transformation: A review of recent observed changes and impacts on biology and human activity. *Reviews of Geophysics* **52**: 185-217.

Miles, M.W., Divine, D.V., et al. 2014. A signal of persistent Atlantic multidecadal variability in Arctic sea ice. *Geophysical Research Letters* **41**: 463-469.

National Snow and Ice Data Center (NSIDC). 2016. *"Charctic" Interactive Sea Ice Graph*. Available online.

Parkinson, C.L. 2014. Spatially mapped reductions in the length of the Arctic sea ice season. *Geophysical Research Letters* **41**: 4316-4322.

Perovich, D., Meier, W., et al. 2015. Sea Ice. Arctic Report Card 2015, NOAA (eds M.O. Jeffries, et al.), pp. 33-40.

Schliebe, S., Rode, K.D., et al. 2008. Effects of sea ice extent and food availability on spatial and temporal distribution of polar bears during the fall open-water period in the southern Beaufort Sea. *Polar Biology* **31**: 999-1010.

Scott, J.B. & Marshall, G.J. 2010. A step-change in the date of sea-ice breakup in western Hudson Bay. *Arctic* **63**: 155-164.

Stern, H.L. and Laidre, K.L. 2016. Sea-ice indicators of polar bear habitat. *Cryosphere* **10**: 2027-2041.

Stirling, I., Lunn, N.J., et al. 2004. Polar bear distribution and abundance on the southwestern Hudson Bay coast during open water season, in relation to population trends and annual ice patterns. *Arctic* **57**: 15-26.

Stroeve, J., Holland, M.M., et al. 2007. Arctic sea ice decline: Faster than forecast. *Geophysical Research Letters* **34**: L09501.

Stroeve, J., Markus, T, et al. 2014. Changes in Arctic melt season and implications for sea ice loss. *Geophysical Research Letters* **41:** 1216-1224.

Vibe, C. 1965. The polar bear in Greenland. In, Proceedings of the 1st International Scientific Meeting on the Polar Bear. 6-10 Sept. 1965, IUCN Polar Bear Specialist Group. U. AK Internat. Conference Proc. Series, No. 1. Washington, pg. 17-25.

Vibe, C. 1967. *Arctic animals in relation to climatic fluctuations.* Meddelelser om Grønland. **170(5)**. C. A. Reitzels Forlag, Copenhagen.

Zhang, X. & Walsh, J.E. 2006. Toward a Seasonally Ice-Covered Arctic Ocean: Scenarios from the IPCC AR4 Model Simulations. *Journal of Climate* **19:** 1730-1747.

Pg. 7 Where females build maternity dens

Amstrup, S.C. 2003. Polar bear (*Ursus maritimus*). In *Wild Mammals of North America,* G.A. Feldhamer, B.C. Thompson and J.A. Chapman (eds), pg. 587-610. Johns Hopkins University Press, Baltimore.

Amstrup, S. & Gardner, C. 1994. Polar bear maternity denning in the Beaufort Sea. *Journal of Wildlife Management* **58:** 1-10.

Bergen, S., Durner, G.M., et al. 2007. Predicting movements of female polar bears between summer sea ice foraging habitats and terrestrial denning habitats of Alaska in the 21st century: proposed methodology and pilot assessment. US Geological Survey. Reston, Virginia.

Derocher, A.E., Andersen, M., et al. 2011. Sea ice and polar bear den ecology at Hopen Island, Svalbard. *Marine Ecology and Progress Series* **441**: 273-279.

Ferguson, S. H., Taylor, M. K., et al. 2000a. Influence of sea ice dynamics on habitat selection by polar bears. *Ecology* **81:** 761-772.

Ferguson, S. H., Taylor, M. K., et al. 2000b. Relationships between denning of polar bears and conditions of sea ice. *Journal of Mammalogy* **81:** 1118-1127.

Messier, F., Taylor, M.K. et al. 1994. Denning ecology of polar bears in the Canadian Arctic Archipelago. *Journal of Mammalogy* **75:** 420-430.

Fischbach, A. S., Amstrup, S. C., et al. 2007. Landward and eastward shift of Alaskan polar bear denning associated with recent sea ice changes. *Polar Biology* **30:** 1395-1405.

Lentfer, J. W. 1975. Polar bear denning on drifting sea ice. *Journal of Mammalogy* **56**: 716-718.

Mauritzen, M., Derocher, A.E., et al. 2001. Space-use strategies of female polar bears in a dynamic sea ice habitat. *Canadian Journal of Zoology* **79:** 1704-1713.

Ovsyanikov, N.G. 2006. Research and conservation of polar bears on Wrangel Island. In Polar Bears: Proceedings of the 14th Working Meeting of the IUCN/SSC Polar Bear Specialist Group, 20-24 June 2005. *Edited by* Aars, J., et al. Occasional Paper of the IUCN Species Survival Commission 32. IUCN, Gland. pp. 167-171.

Ovsyanikov, N. 2010. Polar bear research on Wrangel Island and in the central Arctic Basin. *In* Polar Bears: Proceedings of the 15th meeting of the Polar Bear Specialists Group IUCN/SSC, 29 June-3 July 2009. Occasional Paper of the IUCN Species Survival Commission 43. *Edited by* Obbard, M.E., et al. IUCN Gland. pp. 171-178.

Scott, P.A. & Stirling, I. 2002. Chronology of terrestrial den use by polar bears in western Hudson Bay as indicated by tree growth anomalies. *Arctic* **55:** 151-166.

Stirling, I. & Andriashek, D. 1992. Terrestrial maternity denning of polar bears in the eastern Beaufort Sea area. *Arctic* **45:** 363-366.

Van de Velde (OMI), F., Stirling, I. et al. 2003. Polar bear (*Ursus maritimus*) denning in the area of the Simpson Peninsula, Nunavut. *Arctic* **56:** 191-197.

Zeyl, E., Ehrich, D., et al. 2010. Denning-area fidelity and mitochondrial DNA diversity of female polar bears (*Ursus maritimus*) in the Barents Sea. *Canadian Journal of Zoology* **88**: 1139-1148.

Pg. 9-12 Feast/fast life of polar bears

Amstrup, S.C. 2003. Polar bear (*Ursus maritimus*). In *Wild Mammals of North America*, G.A. Feldhamer, B.C. Thompson and J.A. Chapman (eds), pg. 587-610. Johns Hopkins University Press, Baltimore.

Cameron, M. F., Bengtson, J. L., et al. 2010. Status review of the bearded (*Erignatha barbatus*). NOAA Technical Memorandum NMFS-AFSC-211.

Department of Fisheries and Oceans Canada (DFO). 2014. Status of Northwest Atlantic harp seals, *Pagophilus groenlandicus*. Canadian Science Advisory Secretariat Science Advisory Report 2014/011.

Derocher, A.E. & Stirling, I. 1996. Aspects of survival in juvenile polar bears. *Canadian Journal of Zoology* **73**: 1246–1252.

Derocher, A.E., Stirling, I. et al. 1992. Pregnancy rates and progesterone levels of polar bears in western Hudson Bay. *Canadian Journal of Zoology* **70**: 561–566.

Derocher, A.E., Wiig, Ø., et al. 2002. Diet composition of polar bears in Svalbard and the western Barents Sea. *Polar Biology* **25**: 448–452.

Hammill, M.O. & Smith T.G. 1991. The role of predation in the ecology of the ringed seal in BarrowStrait, Northwest Territories, Canada. *Marine Mammal Science* **7**: 123–135.

Ramsay, M.A. & Stirling, I. 1988. Reproductive biology and ecology of female polar bears (Ursus maritimus). *Journal of Zoology London* **214**: 601-624.

Stirling, I. & Øritsland, N. A. 1995. Relationships between estimates of ringed seal (*Phoca hispida*) and polar bear (*Ursus maritimus*) populations in the Canadian Arctic. *Canadian Journal of Fisheries and Aquatic Science* **52**: 2594 – 2612.

Thiemann, G.W., Iverson, S.J., et al. 2008. Polar bear diets and Arctic marine food webs: insights from fatty acid analysis. *Ecological Monographs* **78**: 591-613.

Whiteman, J.P., Harlow, H.J., et al. 2015. Summer declines in activity and body temperature offer polar bears limited energy savings. *Science* **349**: 295-298.

Pg. 13-14 Evolution

Barnes, I., Matheus, P., et al. 2002. Dynamics of Pleistocene population extinctions in Beringian brown bears. *Science* **295**: 2267-2270.

Cahill JA, Green RE, et al. 2013. Genomic evidence for island population conversion resolves conflicting theories of polar bear evolution. *PLoS Genetics* **9(3)**: e1003345.

Crockford, S.J. 2004. Animal Domestication and Vertebrate Speciation: A Paradigm for the Origin of Species. Ph.D. dissertation, University of Victoria (Canada), Interdisciplinary Studies. [filed at the National Library under Zoology].

Crockford, S.J. 2006. *Rhythms of Life: Thyroid Hormone and the Origin of Species*. Victoria: Trafford.

Crockford, S.J. 2012a. Annotated Map of Ancient Polar Bear Remains of the World. Electronic resource available at https://polarbearscience/references ISBN 978-0-9917966-0-1.

Crockford, S.J. 2012b. Directionality in polar bear hybridization. Comment posted May 1 in response to Edwards et al. 2011. "Ancient hybridization and an Irish origin for the modern polar bear matriline." *Current Biology* **21**: 1251-1258.

Cronin, M.A., Amstrup, S.C. et al. 1991. Interspecific and intraspecific mitochondrial DNA variation in North American bears (*Ursus*). *Canadian Journal of Zoology* **69**: 2985-2992.

Cronin, T. M. & Cronin, M.A. 2015. Biological response to climate change in the Arctic Ocean: the view from the past. *Arktos* **1**: 1-18.

Cronin, M.A., Rincon, G., et al. 2014. Molecular phylogeny and SNP variation of polar bears (*Ursus maritimus*), brown bears (*U. arctos*), and black bears (*U. americanus*) derived from genome sequences. *Journal of Heredity* **105**: 312-323.

Davison, J., Ho, S.Y.W., et al. 2011. Late-Quaternary biogeographic scenarios for the brown bear (Ursus arctos), a wild mammal model species. *Quaternary Science Reviews* **30**: 418-430.

Edwards, C.J., Suchard, M.A., et al. 2011. Ancient hybridization and an Irish origin for the modern polar bear matriline. *Current Biology* **21**: 1251-1258.

Derocher, A.E., Lunn, N.J. et al. 2004. Polar bears in a warming climate. *Integrative and Comparative Biology* **44**: 163–176.

Hailer, F., Kutschera, V.E., et al. 2012. Nuclear genomic sequences reveal that polar bears are an old and distinct bear lineage. *Science* **336**: 344-347.

Heaton, T.H., & Grady, F. 2003. The Late Wisconsin vertebrate history of Prince of Wales Island, Southeast Alaska. In *Ice Age Cave Faunas of North America*, Schubert, B.W., Mead, J.I., Graham, R.W. (eds.), pp.17-53. Indiana University Press, Bloomington.

Heaton, T.H. & Grady, F. 2009. The fossil bears of Southeast Alaska. Proceedings of the 15th International Congress of Speleology 1(1): I-N.

Heaton T.H., Talbot S.L. et al. 1996. An ice age refugium for large mammals in the Alexander Archipelago, southeastern Alaska. *Quaternary Research* **46**: 189–192.

Krause, J., Unger, T., et al. 2008. Mitochondrial genomes reveal an explosive radiation of extinct and extant bears near the Miocene-Pliocene boundary. *BMC Evolutionary Biology* **8**: 220.

Kurtén, B. 1968. *Pleistocene Mammals of Europe*. Weidenfeld and Nicolson, London.

Kurtén, B. & Anderson, E. 1980. *Pleistocene Mammals of North America*. Columbia University Press, New York.

Lindqvist, C., Schuster, S.C., et al. 2010. Complete mitochondrial genome of a Pleistocene jawbone unveils the origin of polar bear. *Proceedings of the National Academy of Sciences USA* **107**: 5053-5057.

Liu, S., Lorenzen, E.D., et al.. 2014. Population genomics reveal recent speciation and rapid evolutionary adaptation in polar bears. *Cell* **157**: 785-794.

Miller, W., Schuster, S.C., et al. 2012. Polar and brown bear genomes reveal ancient admixture and demographic footprints of past climate change. *Proceedings of the National Academy of Sciences USA* **109**: E2382-E2390. doi: 10.1073/pnas.1210506109.

Paetkau, D., Amstrup, S.C., et al. 1999. Genetic structure of the world's polar bear populations. *Molecular Ecology* **8**: 1571–1584.

Pulquério, M. J. F. and R. A. Nichols. 2007. Dates from the molecular clock: how wrong can we be? *Trends in Ecology and Evolution* **22**: 180-184.

Talbot, S.L. & Shields, G.F. 1996a. A phylogeny of the bears (Ursidae) inferred from complete sequences of three mitochondrial DNA genes. *Molecular Phylogeny and Evolution* **5**: 567-575.

Talbot, S.L. & Shields, G.F., 1996b. Phylogeography of brown bears (*Ursus arctos*) of Alaska and paraphyly within the Ursidae. *Molecular Phylogenetics and Evolution* **5**: 477-494.

Pg. 13-14 LGM (and cold periods since)

Bradley, R.S. & England, J.H. 2008. The Younger Dryas and the sea of ancient ice. *Quaternary Research* **70**: 1-10.

Caissie, B. E., Brigham-Grette, J., et al. 2010. Last Glacial Maximum to Holocene sea surface conditions at Umnak Plateau, Bering Sea, as inferred from diatom, alkenone, and stable isotope records. *Paleoceanography* **25**: PA1206.

Clark, P. U., Dyke, A. S., et al. 2009. The Last Glacial Maximum. *Science* **325**: 710-714.

Crockford, S. & Frederick, G. 2007. Sea ice expansion in the Bering Sea during the Neoglacial: evidence from archaeozoology. *The Holocene* **17**: 699-706.

Crockford, S.J. & Frederick, G. 2011. Neoglacial sea ice and life history flexibility in ringed and fur seals. pg.65-91 in T. Braje et al. eds. *Human Impacts on Seals, Sea Lions, and Sea Otters: Integrating Archaeology and Ecology in the Northeast Pacific.* U. California Press, LA.

Crockford, S.J. 2008. Be careful what you ask for: archaeozoological evidence of mid-Holocene climate change in the Bering Sea and implications for the origins of Arctic Thule. Pp. 113-131 in G. Clark, et al. (eds.), *Islands of Inquiry: Colonisation, Seafaring and the Archaeology of Maritime Landscapes.* Terra Australis 29 ANU E Press, Canberra.

Dallimore, A., Enkin, et al. 2008. Postglacial evolution of a Pacific coastal fjord in British Columbia, Canada: interactions of sea-level change, crustal response, and environmental fluctuations — results from MONA core MD02-2494. *Canadian Journal of Earth Science* **45**: 1345-1362.

De Vernal, A. & Hillaire-Marcel, C. 2000. Sea ice cover, sea-surface salinity and halo-/thermocline structure of the northwest North Atlantic: modern versus full glacial conditions. *Quaternary Science Reviews* **12**: 65-85.

Gorbarenko, S. A., Khusid, T.A., et al. 2002. Glacial Holocene environment of the southeastern Okhotsk Sea: evidence from geochemical and palaeontological data. *Palaeogeography, Palaeoclimatology, Palaeoecology* **177**: 237-263.

Hebbeln, D., Henrich, R. et al. 1998. Paleoceanography of the last interglacial/glacial cycle in the polar North Atlantic. *Quaternary Science Reviews* **17**: 125-153.

Hetherington, R., Vaughn-Barrie, J., et al. 2004. Paleogeography, glacially induced crustal displacement, and Late Quaternary coastlines on the continental shelf of British Columbia, Canada. *Quaternary Science Reviews* **23**: 295-318.

Katsuki, K. & Takahashi, K. 2005. Diatoms as paleoenvironmental proxies for seasonal productivity, sea-ice and surface circulation in the Bering Sea during the late Quaternary. *Deep-Sea Research II* **52**: 2110-2130.

Kaufman, D.S. & Manley, W. F. 2004. Pleistocene maximum and Late Wisconsinan glacier extents across Alaska, USA. in J. Ehlers et al. (eds), *Quaternary Glaciation-Extent and Chronology, Part II: North America*, pg. 9-27. Elsevier, Amsterdam.

Mackie, Q., Fedje, D.W., et al. 2011. Early Environments and Archaeology of Coastal British Columbia. In N. F. Bicho, et al. (eds.), *Trekking the Shore: Changing Coastlines and the Antiquity of Coastal Settlement,* pp. 51–103. Interdisciplinary Contributions to Archaeology, Springer, New York.

Mann, D. H. & Hamilton, T. D. 1995. Late Pleistocene and Holocene paleoenvironments of the North Pacific coast. *Quaternary Science Review* **14**: 449-471.

Mann, D. H. & Peteet, D. M. 1994. Extent and timing of the Last Glacial Maximum in southwestern Alaska. *Quaternary Research* **42**: 136-148.

Trend-Staid, M. & Prell, W. L. 2002. Sea surface temperature at the Last Glacial Maximum: A reconstruction using the modern analog technique. *Paleoceanography* **17**: 1065.

Pg. 13-14 Interglacial and Holocene Optimum

Alley, R.B. 2000. The Younger Dryas cold interval as viewed from central Greenland. *Quaternary Science Reviews* **19**: 213-226.

Atkinson, N. 2009. A 10400-year-old bowhead whale (*Balaena mysticetus*) skull from Ellef Ringnes Island, Nunavut: implications for sea-ice conditions in high Arctic Canada at the end of the last glaciation. *Arctic* **62**: 38-44.

CAPE Last Interglacial Project Members, 2006. Last interglacial Arctic warmth confirms polar amplification of climate change. *Quaternary Science Reviews* **25**: 1383-1400.

Condron, A. & Winsor, P. 2012. Meltwater routing and the Younger Dryas. *Proceedings of the National Academy of Science USA.* **109(49)**: 19928–19933.

Cutler, K.B., Edwards, R.L., et al. 2003. Rapid sea-level fall and deep-ocean temperature change since the last interglacial period. *Earth and Planetary Science Letters* **206**: 253-271.

Dredge, L.A. 1992. Field Guide to the Churchill region, Manitoba: Glaciations, sea level changes, permafrost landforms, and archaeology of the Churchill and Gillam areas. Geological Survey of Canada Miscellaneous Report 53.

Dyke, A.S., & England, J.H. 2003. Canada's most northerly postglacial bowhead whales (*Balaena mysticetus*): Holocene sea-ice conditions and polynya development. *Arctic* **56**: 14-20.

Dyke, A. S., Hooper, J. et al. 1996. A history of sea ice in the Canadian Arctic Archipelago based on postglacial remains of bowhead whale (*Balaena mysticetus*). *Arctic* **49**: 235-255.

Dyke, A.S., Hooper, J., et al. 1999. The late Wisconsinan and Holocene record of walrus (*Odobenus rosmarus*) from North America: a review with new data from arctic and Atlantic Canada. *Arctic* **52**: 160-181.

Dyke, A.S., Savelle, J.M. et al. 2011. Paleoeskimo demography and Holocene sea-level history, Gulf of Boothia, Arctic Canada. *Arctic* **64**: 151-168.

Lindqvist, C., Schuster, S.C., et al. 2010. Complete mitochondrial genome of a Pleistocene jawbone unveils the origin of polar bear. *Proceedings of the National Academy of Sciences USA* **107**: 5053-5057.

Miller, W., Schuster, S.C., et al. 2012. Polar and brown bear genomes reveal ancient admixture and demographic footprints of past climate change. *Proceedings of the National Academy of Sciences* **109**: E2382-E2390.

NIPCC 2014. Climate Change Reconsidered II: Biological Implications.

Nichols, H. 1967. Central Canadian palynology and its relevance to Northwestern Europe in the late Quaternary period. *Review of Paleobotany and Palynology* **2**: 231-243.

Polyak, L., Alley, R.B., et al. 2010. History of sea ice in the Arctic. *Quaternary Science Reviews* **29**: 1757-1778.

Thomas, E.K., Briner, J.P. et a. 2016. A major increase in winter snowfall during the middle Holocene on western Greenland caused by reduced sea ice in Baffin Bay and the Labrador Sea. *Geophysical Research Letters* **43(10)**: 5302-5308.

Pg. 15. The great slaughter of polar bears, 1880-1960

Honderich, J.E. 1991. Wildlife as a hazardous resource: an analysis of the historical interaction of humans and polar bears in the Canadian arctic. MA thesis, University of Waterloo, Ontario. [available via university interlibrary loan]

Scott, P.A. & Stirling, I. 2002. Chronology of terrestrial den use by polar bears in western Hudson Bay as indicated by tree growth anomalies. *Arctic* **55**:151-166.

Stirling, I. 2011. *Polar Bears: The Natural History of a Threatened Species*. Fitzhenry & Whiteside, Markham.

Pg. 15. Conservation to 2006 (based on current status)

Anonymous. 1968. Proceedings of the First International Scientific Meeting on the Polar Bear, 6-10 Sept. 1965. University of Alaska International Conference Proceedings Series, No. 1.

Amstrup, S.C. & Wiig, O. (eds.) 1991. Polar Bears: Proceedings of the 10th meeting of the Polar Bear Specialists Group IUCN/SSC, 25-29 Oct. 1988. IUCN, Gland.

Belikov, S.E. 1995. Status of polar bear populations in the Russian Arctic 1993. Polar Bears: Proceedings of the 11th working meeting of the IUCN/SSC Polar Bear Specialists Group, 25-27 Jan. 1993. (eds Ø. Wiig, et al.), Occasional Paper of the IUCN Species Survival Commission, No. 10. IUCN, Gland. Pp. 115-119.

Larsen, T.S. & Stirling, I. 2009. The Agreement on the Conservation of Polar Bears – its History and Future. Norwegian Polar Institute Report 127, Tromso.

Lunn, N.J., Schliebe, S., et al. 2002. Polar Bears: Proceedings of the 13th working meeting of the IUCN/SSC Polar Bear Specialists Group, 23-28 June , 2001. Occasional Paper of the IUCN Species Survival Commission 26. IUCN, Gland.

Pg. 15 Conservation status based on predictions of future survival (after 2006)

Aars, J., Lunn, N. J. et al. 2006. Polar Bears: Proceedings of the 14th Working Meeting of the IUCN/SSC Polar Bear Specialist Group, 20-24 June 2005. Occasional Paper of the IUCN Species Survival Commission 32. IUCN, Gland.

Akçakaya, H.R., Butchart, S.H.M., et al 2006. Use and misuse of the IUCN Red List criteria in projecting climate change impacts on biodiversity. *Global Change Biology* **12:** 2037–2043.

Amstrup, S.C. & Wiig, O. 1991. Polar Bears: Proceedings of the 10th meeting of the Polar Bear Specialists Group IUCN/SSC, 25-29 Oct. 1988. IUCN, Gland.

COSEWIC 2008. Assessment and Update Status Report on the Polar Bear *Ursus maritimus* in Canada. Committee on the Status of Endangered Wildlife in Canada.

Crockford, S.J. 2015. The Arctic Fallacy: Sea Ice Stability and the Polar Bear. *GWPF Briefing* 16. The Global Warming Policy Foundation, London.

Cronin, M.A. 2009. Are polar bears an endangered species? Range Magazine. **Winter:** 40-41.

Cronin, M.A., Amstrup, S.C., et al. 2009. Genetic variation, relatedness, and effective population size of polar bears (Ursus maritimus) in the southern Beaufort Sea, Alaska. *Journal of Heredity* **100:** 681-690.

Derocher, A., Garner, G.W., et al. 1998. Polar Bears: Proceedings of the 12th meeting of the Polar Bear Specialists Group IUCN/SSC, 3-7 February 1997. IUCN, Gland.

Larsen, T.S. & Stirling, I. 2009. *The Agreement on the Conservation of Polar Bears – its History and Future.* Norwegian Polar Institute Report 127, Tromso.

Lowry, L. 2015. *Odobenus rosmarus ssp. divergens.* The IUCN Red List of Threatened Species 2015: e.T61963499A45228901.

Lowry, L. 2016. *Pusa hispida.* The IUCN Red List of Threatened Species 2016: e.T41672A45231341.

Lunn, N.J., Schliebe, S., et al. 2002. Polar Bears: Proceedings of the 13th working meeting of the IUCN/SSC Polar Bear Specialists Group, 23-28 June 2001. IUCN, Gland.

Marine Mammal Commission. 2007. The Marine Mammal Protection Act of 1972, as amended. Compiled and annotated for National Marine Fisheries Service, NOAA, Silver Spring, MD

Obbard, M.E., Theimann, G.W., et al. 2010. Polar Bears: Proceedings of the 15th meeting of the Polar Bear Specialists Group IUCN/SSC, 29 June-3 July 2009. IUCN Gland.

Schliebe, S. Wiig, Ø., et al. 2006a. *Ursus maritimus.* The IUCN Red List of Threatened Species 2006. [see Wiig et al. 2007]

Schliebe, S. Evans, T., et al. 2006b. Range-wide status review of the polar bear *(Ursus maritimus).* Report prepared for the US Fish and Wildlife Service, Anchorage, Alaska.

Wiig, Ø., Born, E.W., et al. 1995. Polar Bears: Proceedings of the 11th working meeting of the IUCN/SSC Polar Bear Specialists Group, 25-27 January 199. IUCN, Gland.

Wiig, Ø., Aars, J., et al. 2007. *Ursus maritimus.* The IUCN Red List of Threatened Species 2007: e.T22823A9390963.

Wiig, Ø., Amstrup, S., et al. 2015. *Ursus maritimus.* The IUCN Red List of Threatened Species 2015: e.T22823A14871490.

York, J., Dowsley, M., et al. 2016. Demographic and traditional knowledge perspectives on the current status of Canadian polar bear subpopulations. *Ecology and Evolution* **6:** 2897-2924.

 US Fish & Wildlife Service. 2008. Determination of threatened status for the polar bear (*Ursus maritimus*) throughout its range. *Federal Register* **73:** 28212-28303.

Vongraven, D., Aars, J., et al.. 2012. A circumpolar monitoring framework for polar bears. *Ursus* **23 (sp2)**: 1-66.

Pg. 16-18 Sea ice predictions

ACIA 2005. Arctic Climate Impact Assessment: Scientific Report. Cambridge University Press.

Amstrup, S.C., Marcot, B.G. et al. 2007. Forecasting the rangewide status of polar bears at selected times in the 21st century. US Geological Survey. Reston, Virginia.

Amstrup, S.C., Marcot, B.G. et al. 2008. A Bayesian network modeling approach to forecasting the 21st century worldwide status of polar bears. *Arctic Sea Ice Decline: Observations, Projections, Mechanisms, and Implications* (eds E.T. DeWeaver, C.M. Bitz & L.B. Tremblay), pp. 213–268. American Geophysical Union Monogr. Ser. No. 180, Washington, D.C.

Douglas, D.C. 2010. *Arctic Sea Ice Decline: Projected Changes in Timing and Extent of Sea Ice in the Bering and Chukchi Seas.* Open-File Report 2010-1176. US Geological Survey. Reston, Virginia.

Durner, G.M., Douglas, D.C., et al. 2006. A model for autumn pelagic distribution of female polar bears in the Chukchi Sea, 1987-1994. US Geological Survey. Reston, Virginia.

Durner, G.M., Douglas, D.C., et al. 2007. Predicting 21st-century polar bear habitat distribution from global climate models. US Geological Survey. Reston, Virginia.

Durner, G.M., Douglas, D.C., et al. 2009. Predicting 21st-century polar bear habitat distribution from global climate models. *Ecology Monographs* **79**: 25–58.

Furevik, T., Drange, H., et al. 2002. Anticipated changes in the Nordic Seas marine climate: Scenarios for 2020, 2050, and 2080. *Fisken og Havet* 2002-4: 1-13.

Hassol, S.J. 2004. Impacts of a Warming Arctic: Arctic Climate Impact Assessment Synthesis Report. Cambridge University Press, Cambridge UK. [summary for policy makers published ahead of the report containing the science background]

Hunter, C.M., Caswell, H., et al. 2007. Polar bears in the Southern Beaufort Sea II: Demography and population growth in relation to sea ice conditions. US Geological Survey. Reston.

IPCC 2007. Climate Change 2007: The Physical Science Basis. Contribution of Working Group I to the Fourth Assessment Report of the Intergovernmental Panel on Climate Change. Cambridge University Press, Cambridge.

Overland, J.E. and Wang, M. 2013. When will the summer Arctic be nearly sea ice-free? *Geophysical Research Letters* **40**: 2097–2101.

Wang, M. & Overland, J.E. 2015. Projected future duration of the sea-ice-free season in the Alaskan Arctic. *Progress in Oceanography* **136**: 50-59.

Pg. 17 Polar bear population predictions

Amstrup, S.C., Marcot, B.G. et al. 2007. Forecasting the rangewide status of polar bears at selected times in the 21st century. US Geological Survey. Reston, VA.

Amstrup, S.C., Marcot, B.G. et al. 2008. A Bayesian network modeling approach to forecasting the 21st century worldwide status of polar bears. *Arctic Sea Ice Decline: Observations, Projections, Mechanisms, and Implications* (eds E.T. DeWeaver, C.M. Bitz & L.B. Tremblay), pp. 213–268. American Geophysical Union Monogr. Ser. No. 180, Washington, DC.

Amstrup, S.C., DeWeaver, E.T., et al. 2010. Greenhouse gas mitigation can reduce sea-ice loss and increase polar bear persistence. *Nature* **468**: 955–958.

Bergen, S., Durner, G.M., et al. 2007. Predicting movements of female polar bears between summer sea ice foraging habitats and terrestrial denning habitats of Alaska in the 21st century: proposed methodology and pilot assessment. US Geological Survey. Reston, VA.

Courtland, R. 2008. Polar bear numbers set to fall. *Nature* **453**: 432-433.

Derocher, A.E., Aars, J., et al. 2013. Rapid ecosystem change and polar bear conservation. *Conservation Letters* **6**:368-375.

Hunter, C.M., Caswell, H., et al. 2007. Polar bears in the southern Beaufort Sea II: demography and population growth in relation to sea ice conditions, 2001-2006. Administrative Report US Geological Survey, Reston, VA.

Kelly, B., Whiteley, A., et al. 2010. Comment: The Arctic melting pot. *Nature* **468**: 891.

Obbard, M.E., McDonald, T.L., et al 2007. Polar bear population status in southern Hudson Bay, Canada. Administrative Report, U.S. Department of the Interior- U.S. Geological Survey, Reston, VA.

Post, E., Bhatt, U.S., et al. 2013. Ecological consequences of sea-ice decline. *Science* **341**: 519-524.

Regehr, E.V., Hunter, C.M., et al. 2007a. Polar bears in the Southern Beaufort Sea I: Survival and breeding in relation to sea ice conditions. US Geological Survey. Reston, VA.

Regehr, E.V., Lunn, N.J., et al. 2007b. Effects of earlier sea ice breakup on survival and population size of polar bears in Western Hudson Bay. *Journal of Wildlife Management* **71**: 2673-2683.

Rode, K. D., Amstrup, S.C. et al. 2007. Polar bears in the Southern Beaufort Sea III: Stature, mass, and cub recruitment in relationship to time and sea ice extent between 1982 and 2006. US Geological Survey. Reston, VA.

Stirling, I. & Derocher, A.E. 2012. Effects of climate warming on polar bears: a review of the evidence. *Global Change Biology* **18**: 2694–2706.

Stirling, I. and Parkinson, C.L. 2006. Possible effects of climate warming on selected populations of polar bears (*Ursus maritimus*) in the Canadian Arctic. *Arctic* **59**: 261–275.

Stirling, I., Lunn, N.J., et al. 1999. Long-term trends in the population ecology of polar bears in Western Hudson Bay in relation to climate change. *Arctic* **52**: 294-306.

Stirling, I., Lunn, N.J., et al. 2004. Polar bear distribution and abundance on the southwestern Hudson Bay coast during open water season, in relation to population trends and annual ice patterns. *Arctic* **57**: 15–26.

Pg. 18-20. Evidence for thriving and stable subpopulations

Atwood, T.C., Peacock, E., et al. 2016. Rapid environmental change drives increased land use by an Arctic marine predator. *PLoS One* **11(6)**: e0155932. doi:10.1371/journal.pone.0155932.

Berghund, N. 2015. Polar bears make a surprise comeback. *Newsinenglish*, December 24, 2015. Available from http://www.newsinenglish.no/2015/12/24/polar-bears-make-a-comeback/ [accessed May 22, 2016]

Castro de la Guardia, L., Myers, P.G. et a. 2017. Sea ice cycle in western Hudson Bay, Canada, from a polar bear perspective. *Marine Ecology Progress Series* in press. DOI 10.3354/meps11964.

Cherry, S.G., Derocher, A.E., et al. 2016. Habitat-mediated timing of migration in polar bears: an individual perspective. *Ecology and Evolution* in press. doi 10.1002/ece3.2233

Cherry, S.G., Derocher, A.E., et al. 2013. Migration phenology and seasonal fidelity of an Arctic marine predator in relation to sea ice dynamics. *Journal of Animal Ecology* **82**: 912–921.

Crawford, J. & Quakenbush, L. 2013. *Ringed seals and climate change: early predictions versus recent observations in Alaska.* Presentation by Justin Crawfort, 28th Lowell Wakefield Fisheries Symposium, March 26–29, Anchorage, AK. Online.

Crawford, J.A., Quakenbush, L.T. et al. 2015. A comparison of ringed and bearded seal diet, condition and productivity between historical (1975–1984) and recent (2003–2012) periods in the Alaskan Bering and Chukchi seas. *Progress in Oceanography* **136:** 133-150.

Crockford, S.J. 2017. Testing the hypothesis that routine sea ice coverage of 3-5 mkm2 results in a greater than 30% decline in population size of polar bears (*Ursus maritimus*). *PeerJ Preprints* 2 March 2017. Doi: 10.7287/peerj.preprints.2737v3

Cronin, M.A., Amstrup, S.C., et al. 2009. Genetic variation, relatedness, and effective population size of polar bears (*Ursus maritimus*) in the southern Beaufort Sea, Alaska. *Journal of Heredity* **100:** 681-690.

Galicia, M.P., Thiemann, G.W., et al. 2016. Dietary habits of polar bears in Foxe Basin, Canada: possible evidence of a trophic regime shift mediated by a new top predator. *Ecology and Evolution* in press. doi: 10.1002/ece3.2173

Lunn, N.J., Servanty, S., et al. 2016. Demography of an apex predator at the edge of its range – impacts of changing sea ice on polar bears in Hudson Bay. *Ecological Applications* **26:** 1302-1320.

Matishov, G.G., Chelintsev, N.G., et al. 2014. Assessment of the amount of polar bears (*Ursus maritimus*) on the basis of perennial vessel counts. *Doklady Earth Sciences* **458 (2):** 1312-1316.

Norwegian Polar Institute 2015. Polar *bears in Svalbard in good condition – so far.* Press release 23 December 2015. Available from http://www.npolar.no/en/news/2015/12-23-counting-of-polar-bears-in-svalbard.html [accessed July 1, 2016].

Obbard, M.E., Middel, K.R., et al. 2015. Estimating abundance of the Southern Hudson Bay polar bears subpopulation using aerial surveys. *Polar Biology* **38:** 1713-1725.

Obbard, M.E., Cattet, M.R.I., et al. 2016. Trends in body condition in polar bears (*Ursus maritimus*) from the Southern Hudson Bay subpopulation in relation to changes in sea ice. *Arctic Science* **2:** 15-32.

Peacock, E., Taylor, M.K., et al. 2013. Population ecology of polar bears in Davis Strait, Canada and Greenland. *Journal of Wildlife Management* **77:** 463–476.

Pongracz, J.D. & Derocher, A.E. 2016. Summer refugia of polar bears (*Ursus maritimus*) in the southern Beaufort Sea. *Polar Biology* in press. doi 10.1007/s00300-016-1997-8

Rode, K. & Regehr, E.V. 2010. Polar bear research in the Chukchi and Bering Seas: A synopsis of 2010 field work. Unpublished report to the US Fish and Wildlife Service, Dept. Interior, Anchorage.

Rode, K.D., Peacock, E., et al. 2012. A tale of two polar bear populations: ice habitat, harvest and body condition. *Population Ecology* **54:** 3–18.

Rode, K.D., Regehr, E.V., et al. 2014. Variation in the response of an Arctic top predator experiencing habitat loss: feeding and reproductive ecology of two polar bear populations. *Global Change Biology* **20:** 76–88.

Rode, K.D., Wilson, R.R., et al. 2015. Increased land use by Chukchi Sea polar bears in relation to changing sea ice conditions. *PLoS One* **10:** e0142213.

Rogers, M.C., Peacock, E., et al. 2015. Diet of female polar bears in the southern Beaufort Sea of Alaska: evidence for an emerging alternative foraging strategy in response to environmental change. *Polar Biology* **38:** 1035-1047.

Sahanatien V. & Derocher A.E. 2012. Monitering sea ice habitat fragmentation for polar bear conservation. *Animal Conservation* **15:** 397-406.

Stapleton S., Atkinson, S., et al. 2014. Revisiting Western Hudson Bay: using aerial surveys to update polar bear abundance in a sentinel population. *Biological Conservation* **170:** 38-47.

Stapleton, S., Peacock, E. et al. 2016. Aerial surveys suggest long-term stability in the seasonally ice-free Foxe Basin (Nunavut) polar bear population. *Marine Mammal Science* **32:** 181-201.

SWG [Scientific Working Group to the Canada-Greenland Joint Commission on Polar Bear. 2016. Re-Assessment of the Baffin Bay and Kane Basin Polar Bear Subpopulations: http://www.gov.nu.ca/documents-publications/349

Viengkone, M., Derocher, A.E., et al. 2016. Assessing polar bear (*Ursus maritimus*) population structure in the Hudson Bay region using SNPs. *Ecology and Evolution* in press. DOI:10.1002/ece3.2563.

Wilson, R.R., Regehr, E.V., et al. 2016. Invariant polar bear habitat selection during a period of sea ice loss. *Proceedings of the Royal Society B* **283**: 20160380.

Whiteman, J.P., Harlow, H.J., et al. 2015. Summer declines in activity and body temperature offer polar bears limited energy savings. *Science* **349**: 295-298.

York, J., Dowsley, M., et al. 2016. Demographic and traditional knowledge perspectives on the current status of Canadian polar bear subpopulations. *Ecology and Evolution* **6**: 2897-2924.

Pg. 21 Evidence for thick ice development in the Beaufort Sea and Hudson Bay

Bromaghin, J.F., McDonald, T.L., et al. 2015. Polar bear population dynamics in the southern Beaufort Sea during a period of sea ice decline. *Ecological Applications* **25**: 634-651.

Burns, J. J., Fay, F. H., et al. 1975. The relationships of marine mammal distributions, densities, and activities to sea ice conditions (Quarterly report 1975), pp. 77-78 in Environmental Assessment of the Alaskan Continental Shelf, Principal Investiagors' Reports. July-September 1975, Volume 1. NOAA, Environmental Research Laboratories, Boulder Colorado.

Chambellant, M., Stirling, I., et al. 2012. Temporal variations in Hudson Bay ringed seal (*Phoca hispida*) life-history parameters in relation to environment. *Journal of Mammalogy* **93**: 267-281.

Crockford, S.J. 2015. The Arctic Fallacy: Sea Ice Stability and the Polar Bear. *GWPF Briefing* 16. The Global Warming Policy Foundation, London.

Harwood, L.A., Smith, T.G. et al. 2000. Variation in reproduction and body condition of the ringed seal (Phoca hispida) in western Prince Albert Sound, NT, Canada, as assessed through a harvest-based sampling program. *Arctic* **53**: 422 – 431.

Harwood, L.A., Smith, T.G., et al. 2012. Ringed seals and sea ice in Canada's western Arctic: harvest-based monitoring 1992–2011. *Arctic* **65**: 377–390.

Harwood, L.A. and Stirling. I. 1992. Distribution of ringed seals in the southeastern Beaufort Sea during late summer. *Canadian Journal of Zoology* **70**: 891-900.

Lentfer 1976. Polar bear management and research in Alaska 1974-76. Pg. 187-197 in [Anonymous]. Polar Bears: Proceedings of the 6th meeting of the Polar Bear Specialists Group IUCN/SSC, 7 December, 1976, Morges, Switzerland. Gland, Switzerland and Cambridge UK, IUCN.

Pilfold, N.W., Derocher, A.E., et al. 2014. Polar bear predatory behaviour reveals seascape distribution of ringed seal lairs. *Population Ecology* **56**: 129-138.

Pilfold, N. W., Derocher, A. E., et al. 2015. Multi-temporal factors influence predation for polar bears in a changing climate. *Oikos* **124**: 1098-1107.

Pilfold, N.W., McCall, A. et al. 2016. Migratory response of polar bears to sea ice loss: to swim or not to swim. *Ecography* 39 in press DOI: 10.1111/ecog.02109.

Stirling, I. 2002. Polar bears and seals in the eastern Beaufort Sea and Amundsen Gulf: a synthesis of population trends and ecological relationships over three decades. *Arctic* **55** (Suppl. 1): 59-76.

Stirling, I., Andriashek, D., et al. 1975a. Distribution and abundance of polar bears in the Eastern Beaufort Sea. Beaufort Sea Tech. Report #2, Dept. Environment, Victoria, B.C.

Stirling, I., Andriashek, D., et al. 1988. Assessment of the polar bear population in the eastern Beaufort Sea. Final Report to the Northern Oil and Gas Assessment Program. Canadian Wildlife Service, Edmonton, Alberta, Canada. 81 pp.

Stirling, I., Archibald, R. et al. 1975b. Distribution and abundance of seals in the Eastern Beaufort Sea. Beaufort Sea Tech. Report #1, Dept. Environment, Victoria, B.C.

Stirling, I. &Archibald, W.R. 1977. Aspects of predation of seals by polar bears. *Journal of the Fisheries Board of Canada* **34:** 1126–1129.

Stirling, I, Cleator, H. et al. 1981. Marine mammals. In: Polynyas in the Canadian Arctic, Stirling, I. and Cleator, H. (eds), pg. 45-58. Canadian Wildlife Service Occasional Paper No. 45. Ottawa.

Stirling, I. & Derocher, A.E. 2012. Effects of climate warming on polar bears: a review of the evidence. *Global Change Biology* **18:** 2694-2706.

Stirling, I, Kingsley, M. et al. 1982. The distribution and abundance of seals in the eastern Beaufort Sea, 1974–79. Canadian Wildlife Service Occasional Paper 47. Edmonton.

Stirling, I. & Lunn, N.J. 1997. Environmental fluctuations in arctic marine ecosystems as reflected by variability in reproduction of polar bears and ringed seals. In *Ecology of Arctic Environments*, Woodin, S.J. et al. (eds), pg. 167-181. Blackwell Science, UK.

Stirling, I., Schweinsburg, R.E., et al. 1980. Research on polar bears in Canada 1976-78. *In* Polar Bears: Proceedings of the 7th meeting of the Polar Bear Specialists Group IUCN/SSC, 30 Jan.-1 Feb. 1979. *Eds.* Anonymous. IUCN, Gland. pp. 45–53.

Stirling, I., Schweinsburg, R.E., et al. 1985. Research on polar bears in Canada 1978-80. Polar Bears: Proceedings of the 8th meeting of the Polar Bear Specialists Group IUCN/SSC, 15-19 Jan. 1981. (ed Anonymous), pp. 71-98. IUCN, Gland.

Stirling, I., Richardson, E., et al. 2008. Unusual predation attempts of polar bears on ringed seals in the southern Beaufort Sea: possible significance of changing spring ice conditions. *Arctic* **61:** 14–22.

Pg. 21-25 Effects of thick spring ice on ringed seals and polar bears

Amstrup, S.C., Stirling, I., et al. 2006. Recent observations of intraspecific predation and cannibalism among polar bears in the Southern Beaufort Sea. *Polar Biology* **29**: 997–1002.

Cherry, S.G., Derocher, A.E., et al. 2009. Fasting physiology of polar bears in relation to environmental change and breeding behavior in the Beaufort Sea. *Polar Biology* **32**: 383-391

Harwood, L.A., Smith, T.G., et al. 2012. Ringed seals and sea ice in Canada's western Arctic: harvest-based monitoring 1992-2011. *Arctic* **65:** 377-390.

Pilfold, N.W., Derocher, A.E., et al. 2012. Age and sex composition of seals killed by polar bears in the eastern Beaufort Sea. *PLoS ONE* 7:e41429. Doi:10.1371/journal.pone.0041429.

Regehr, E.V., Hunter, C.M., et al. 2010. Survival and breeding of polar bears in the southern Beaufort Sea in relation to sea ice. *Journal of Animal Ecology* **79:** 117–127.

Rode, K.D., Amstrup, S.C., et al. 2010. Reduced body size and cub recruitment in polar bears associated with sea ice decline. *Ecological Applications* **20:** 768-782.

Rode, K.D., Douglas, D., et al. 2013. Comparison in polar bear response to sea ice loss in the Chukchi and southern Beaufort Seas. Oral presentation at the *28th Lowell Wakefield Fisheries Symposium,* March 26-29. Anchorage, AK.

Rode, K. & Regehr, E.V. 2010. Polar bear research in the Chukchi and Bering Seas: A synopsis of 2010 field work. Unpublished report to the US Fish and Wildlife Service, Department of the Interior, Anchorage.

Rode, K.D., Regher, E.V. et al. 2014. Variation in the response of an Arctic top predator experiencing habitat loss: feeding and reproductive ecology of two polar bear populations. *Global Change Biology* **20:** 76-88.

Smith, T.G. 1987. The Ringed Seal, *Phoca hispida*, of the Canadian Western Arctic. *Canadian Bulletin of Fisheries and Aquatic Sciences 216*. Department of Fisheries and Oceans, Ottawa.

Smith T.G. & Stirling I. 1975. The breeding habitat of the ringed seal (*Phoca hispida*), the birth lair and associated structures. *Canadian Journal of Zoology* **53:** 1297-1305.

Stirling, I. 1997. The importance of polynyas, ice edges, and leads to marine mammals and birds. *Journal of Marine Systems* **10**: 9-21.

Stirling, I. 2002. Polar bears and seals in the eastern Beaufort Sea and Amundsen Gulf: a synthesis of population trends and ecological relationships over three decades. *Arctic* **55 (Suppl. 1)**: 59-76.

Stirling, I., Andriashek, D., et al. 1975. Distribution and abundance of polar bears in the Eastern Beaufort Sea. Beaufort Sea Tech. Report #2, Dept. Environment, Victoria, B.C.

Stirling, I., Archibald, R. et al. 1975. Distribution and abundance of seals in the Eastern Beaufort Sea. Beaufort Sea Tech. Report #1, Dept. Environment, Victoria, B.C.

Stirling, I, Cleator, H. et al. 1981. Marine mammals. *Polynyas in the Canadian Arctic* (eds I. Stirling & H. Cleator), pp. 45-58. Canadian Wildlife Service Occasional Paper No. 45. Ottawa.

Stirling, I. and Derocher, A.E. 2013. Effects of climate warming on polar bears: a review of the evidence. *Global Change Biology* **18 (9)**: 2694-2706 doi:10.1111/j.1365-2486.2012.02753.x

Stirling, I. & Lunn, N.J. 1997. Environmental fluctuations in arctic marine ecosystems as reflected by variability in reproduction of polar bears and ringed seals. In *Ecology of Arctic Environments*, Woodin, S.J. and Marquiss, M. (eds), pg. 167-181. Blackwell Science, UK.

Stirling, I., Andriashek, D., et al. 1993. Habitat preferences of polar bears in the western Canadian Arctic in late winter and spring. *Polar Record* **29**:13-24.

Stirling, I., McDonald, T.L., et al. 2011. Polar bear population status in the northern Beaufort Sea, Canada, 1971-2006. *Ecological Applications* **21**: 859-876.

Stirling, I., Richardson, E., et al. 2008. Unusual predation attempts of polar bears on ringed seals in the southern Beaufort Sea: possible significance of changing spring ice conditions. *Arctic* **61**: 14-22.

Stirling, I., Schweinsburg, R.E., et al. 1980. Proceedings of the 7th meeting of the Polar Bear Specialists Group IUCN/SSC, 30 January-1 February, 1979, Copenhagen, Denmark. Gland, Switzerland and Cambridge UK, IUCN., pg. 45-53.

Pg. 25-26 Effects of variable snow cover on ringed seals and polar bears

Calvert, W., Stirling, I., et al. 1986. Polar bear management in Canada 1982-84. In: Polar Bears: Proceedings of the 9th meeting of the Polar Bear Specialists Group IUCN/SSC, 9-11 Aug. 1985, Anonymous (eds). IUCN, Gland. Pg. 19-34.

Chambellant, M., Stirling, I., et al. 2012. Temporal variations in Hudson Bay ringed seal (*Phoca hispida*) life-history parameters in relation to environment. *Journal of Mammalogy* **93**: 267-281.

Derocher, A.E. & Stirling, I. 1996. Aspects of survival in juvenile polar bears. *Canadian Journal of Zoology* **73**: 1246-1252.

Ferguson, S.H., Stirling, I., et al. 2005. Climate change and ringed seal (*Phoca hispida*) recruitment in Western Hudson Bay. *Marine Mammal Science* **21**: 121-135.

Hammill, M.O. & Smith T.G. 1991. The role of predation in the ecology of the ringed seal in Barrow Strait, Northwest Territories, Canada. *Marine Mammal Science* **7**: 123–135.

Hezel, P.J., Zhang,X., et al. 2012. Projected decline in spring snow depth on Arctic sea ice caused by progressively later autumn open ocean freeze-up this century. *Geophysical Research Letters* **39**: L17505, doi:10.1029/2012GL052794.

Holst, M., Stirling, I. et al. 1999. Age structure and reproductive rates of ringed seals (*Phoca hispida*) on the northwest coast of Hudson Bay in 1991 and 1992. *Marine Mammal Science* **15**: 1357-1364.

Kwok, R., Panzer, B., et al. 2011. Airborne surveys of snow depth over Arctic sea ice. *Journal of Geophysical Research* **116**: C11018, doi:10.1029/2011JC007371.

Lunn, N.J., Servanty, S., et al. 2016. Demography of an apex predator at the edge of its range – impacts of changing sea ice on polar bears in Hudson Bay. *Ecological Applications* **26**: 1302-1320.

Martinez-Bakker, M.E., Sell, S.K., et al. 2013. Combined genetic and telemetry data reveal high rates of gene flow, migration, and long-distance dispersal potential in Arctic ringed seals (*Pusa hispida*). PLoS One **8**: e77125.

Pilfold, N.W., Derocher, A.E., et al. 2014. Polar bear predatory behaviour reveals seascape distribution of ringed seal lairs. *Population Ecology* **56**: 129-138.

Pilfold, N. W., Derocher, A. E., et al. 2015. Multi-temporal factors influence predation for polar bears in a changing climate. *Oikos* **124**: 1098-1107.

Ramseier, R.O., Vant, M.R., et al. 1975. Distribution of the ice thickness in the Beaufort Sea. Beaufort Sea Technical Report #30. Canada Dept. of Environment, Victoria, B.C.

Ramsay, M.A. & Stirling, I. 1988. Reproductive biology and ecology of female polar bears (*Ursus maritimus*). *Journal of Zoology London* **214**: 601-624.

Smith, T.G. & Stirling, I. 1975. The breeding habitat of the ringed seal (*Phoca hispida*): the birth lair and associated structures. *Canadian Journal of Zoology* **53**: 1297-1305.

Stirling, I. & Derocher, A.E. 2012. Effects of climate warming on polar bears: a review of the evidence. *Global Change Biology* **18**: 2694-2706.

Stirling, I., Lunn, N.J. et al. 1999. Long-term trends in the population ecology of polar bears in Western Hudson Bay in relation to climate change. **Arctic 52**: 294-306.

Stirling, I. & Parkinson, C.L. 2006. Possible effects of climate warming on selected populations of polar bears (*Ursus maritimus*) in the Canadian Arctic. *Arctic* **59**: 261-275.

Stirling, I. & Smith, T.G. 2004. Implications of warm temperatures and an unusual rain event for the survival of ringed seals on the coast of southeastern Baffin Island. *Arctic* **57**: 59–67.

Taylor, K.E., Stouffer, R.J. et al. 2012. An overview of CMIP5 and the experiment design. *Bulletin of the American Meteorological Society* **93**: 485-498.

Pg. 29 Conclusions

Atwood, T.C., Marcot, B.G., et a. 2016. Forecasting the relative influence of environmental and anthropogenic stressors on polar bears. *Ecosphere* **7**: e01370. 10.1002/ecs2.1370

Crockford, S.J. 2017. Testing the hypothesis that routine sea ice coverage of 3-5 mkm2 results in a greater than 30% decline in population size of polar bears (*Ursus maritimus*). *PeerJ Preprints* 2 March 2017. Doi: 10.7287/peerj.preprints.2737v3

Laidre K.L., Stern, H. et al. 2015. Arctic marine mammal population status, sea ice habitat loss, and conservation recommendations for the 21st century. *Conservation Biology* **29**: 724–737.

Regehr, E.V., Laidre, K.L., et al. 2016. Conservation status of polar bears (*Ursus maritimus*) in relation to projected sea-ice declines. *Biology Letters* **12**: 20160556.

US Fish & Wildlife Service (USFWS). 2011. 12-month finding on a petition to list the Pacific walrus as endangered or threatened. *Federal Register* **76**: 7634–7676.

US Fish & Wildlife Service (USFWS). 2012a. Threatened status for the Arctic, Okhotsk and Baltic subspecies of the ringed seal. *Federal Register* **77**: 76706–76738.

US Fish & Wildlife Service (USFWS). 2012b. Threatened status for the Beringia and Okhotsk distinct population segments of the *Erignathus barbatus nauticus* subspecies of the bearded seal. *Federal Register* **77**: 76740–76768.

Photo & Figure Credits

Front cover, US Fish & Wildlife Service, Barrow.
Back cover, Shutterstock, purchased license.
Frontspiece, Shutterstock, purchased license.
Pg i, Alexandria Fredrick, commissioned headshot; Free clipart.
Pg ii, Gary Kramer, US Fish & Wildlife Service, 2006.
Fig. 1, US National Snow & Ice Data Service, labels added, 27 February 2015.
Fig. 2, Wikipedia Creative Commons license, labels added.
Fig. 3, Environment Canada, labels added.
Fig. 4, US National Snow & Ice Data Service, 14 April 2015.
Fig. 5, US National Snow & Ice Data Service, 11 September 2016.
Fig. 6, Wikipedia Creative Commons license.
Fig. 7, US Geological Survey.
Fig. 8, Steve Hillebrand, US Fish & Wildlife Service.
Fig. 9, Brendan Kelly, US NOAA (left) and Shutterstock, purchased license (right).
Fig. 10, Susan Crockford, PolarBearScience.
Fig. 11, Wikipedia Creative Commons license.
Fig. 12, Suzanne Miller, US Fish & Wildlife Service (left) and Shutterstock, purchased license (right).
Fig. 13, Wikipedia Creative Commons license, labels added by JF Baichtal and SJ Crockford, with permission.
Fig. 14a, Arctic Climate Impact Assessment, open access.
Fig. 14b, US National Snow & Ice Data Service, 10 September 2012.
Fig. 15, US Geological Survey.
Fig. 16, Shutterstock, purchased license.
Fig. 17, Wikipedia Creative Commons license.
Fig. 18, GRID Arendal, open access, labels added.
Fig. 19, US Geological Survey (left) and US Navy (right).
Fig. 20, Wikipedia Creative Commons license.
Fig. 21, Steven Amstrup, US Geological Survey.
Fig. 22, Shutterstock, purchased license.
Pg . 47, Shutterstock, purchased license.

Glossary

IUCN – International Union for the Conservation of Nature

PBSG – Polar Bear Specialist Group

USGS – United States (of America) Geological Survey [a federal government department]

USFWS – United States (of America) Fish & Wildlife Service [a federal government department]

IPCC – Intergovernmental Panel on Climate Change

DNA – refers to the genetic material found in living cells

Pleistocene – the last geological age (about 2.6 million – 11,500/11,700 years before present)

Present – in carbon dating, refers to a standard reference time of 1950

Glacial – thousands of years of intensely cold climate when polar and mountain glacier ice expanded

Interglacial – thousands of years of globally warm climate between glacial periods.

LGM – Last Glacial Maximum, aka Last Ice Age (26,000-11,500/11,700 years before present)

Holocene – the latest stage of the Quaternary, which began about 11,500/11,700 years before present

Quaternary Period – Pleistocene plus the Holocene

Holocene Climate Maximum – a relatively long warm period, 11,500/11,700-8,500 years before present

Eemian – aka Sangamonian, last warm Interglacial (about 130,000-110,000 years before present)

NSIDC – US National Snow and Ice Data Center [a federal government department]

mkm² – million kilometers squared [area of sea ice coverage]

perennial sea ice – ice that does not melt completely in winter

multiyear ice – see 'perennial' ice, refers to ice (by number of years old) that survived the last summer

annual ice – aka first year ice, refers to ice that melts completely over the summer

sea ice extent – a measure calculated to the perimeter edge of a particular concentration (i.e. 15% or 50%)

Acknowledgements

Special thanks to Hilary Ostrov for copy editing and to the many lecture audiences in Victoria who provided the inspiration for this book. This work is based on several published and unpublished peer-reviewed papers, as well as blog posts I have written over the years that have garnered feedback from experts in various fields. While I have endeavored to be as accurate as possible, a few typos may have slipped through, for which I take full responsibility.

Made in the
USA
Monee, IL